Praise for *The Way We Survive*

'Honest and unapologetic, Catriona Morton's book brings nuance and poignant personal insight to a topic which is more than just 'timely' – sexual violence is a lived a reality for many of us in society, and has always been. In so doing, she offers a guiding hand for any victim or survivor out there who has felt lost, isolated, or misunderstood. A book that builds community and understanding'
Winnie M Li, author of *Complicit*

'A luminous, empathetic, inclusive and urgent book. This book taught me so much about trauma and survival, about the world, and about myself. Catriona's voice is clear and lucid and it is a lifeline to survivors everywhere and those who love them. I am so grateful for this book and I will return to it again and again. Everyone should read it'
Lucia Osborne-Crowley,
author of *My Body Keeps Your Secrets*

'One of the most important, impressive and compassionate books I've read on surviving sexual violence. *The Way We Survive* perfectly blends the personal with the political to create a series of raw, honest, moving and well-researched essays. This book helped me enormously in understanding my own CPTSD. I'm so glad I found it'
Katy Wix, author of *Delicacy*

# THE WAY WE SURVIVE

## SURVIVE

### Notes on Rape Culture

## Catriona Morton

First published in Great Britain in 2021 by Trapeze,
This paperback edition published in 2022 by Trapeze,
an imprint of The Orion Publishing Group Ltd
Carmelite House, 50 Victoria Embankment,
London EC4Y ODZ

An Hachette UK company

1 3 5 7 9 10 8 6 4 2

A CIP catalogue record for this book is
available from the British Library.

ISBN (Mass Market Paperback): 978 1 398 70056 7
ISBN (eBook): 978 1 398 70057 4
ISBN (Audio): 978 1 398 70082 6

Typeset by Born Group
Printed and bound in Great Britain by Clays Ltd, Elcograf S.p.A.

MIX
Paper from
responsible sources
FSC® C104740

www.orionbooks.co.uk

For all the survivors who came before me, and all those who will come after.

'My silences had not protected me. Your silences will not protect you'

Audre Lorde

'Do not become the ones who hurt you. Stay tender with your power'

Chanel Miller

'The only way to survive is by taking care of one another'

Grace Lee Boggs

# Contents

# A Note on the Title

This book denotes the way I have survived through my own experiences of sexual violence and explores various aspects of our rape culture. I want to remind us all that not everyone survives sexual violence – whether they are murdered in the attack or whether they die from the after-effects.

This book is for survivors, but it also remembers those survivors and victims who didn't survive.

# Author's Note

During the publication process for this book, the manuscript was read by a lawyer to assess the text for any risks it might present, particularly in relation to defamation. This process was primarily to ensure that I hadn't implied guilt or made accusations against any individual who hasn't already been found guilty of such crimes in a court of law. To do so would illegally damage the accused's public reputation and applies to the reader's ability to identify them explicitly as well as to something called jigsaw identification, whereby readers could piece together the identity of the accused with small, seemingly insignificant details. As such, there are certain things I am not legally permitted to say or write about, both relating to my own abuses as well as the experiences of others. My voice has been moderated, moulded, and in some cases silenced by the need to adhere to the legal system we currently live in.

This is a reality for anyone talking publicly about abuses they've suffered. I wish I could tell you the truth in its entirety, but that isn't possible.

Upon reading this book, and other accounts of serious violence, I invite you to read with an inquisitive mind – perhaps asking what's missing, why things must be worded in certain, careful ways, and, perhaps most pertinently, about the stories we'll never get to hear.

# Trigger Warnings

Trigger warnings are vital because they are about accessibility. I want this book to be as accessible as possible for those who want it in their life. These trigger warnings are here to equip readers who need them to stay safe. To quote the disability activist and writer Eli Clare, 'without trigger warnings many of us would lose access to conversations, communities and learning spaces'. I want to try my hardest to keep this access possible.

This book will talk, almost constantly, about rape and sexual assault, childhood sexual abuse – as well as a plethora of actions and experiences on what we call 'the continuum of sexual violence' – and the after-effects of such violence. It also discusses various prejudices and violences in the world, such as transphobia, homophobia, racism and ableism. My story itself may trigger you, or it might be something completely random that acts as a trigger. By 'trigger', I mean remind you, in any sense – physically, psychologically, emotionally – of something bad you experienced in the past.

You may be ready to relive the feelings of this trauma, or you may not be. I urge you to gently care for yourself whilst reading this. Take it as slowly as you want; read it for a whole day straight and then don't look at it for six months; read a paragraph a week; read it and be angry or upset with the world, or even with me. Do whatever you need to do to feel safe and held. That might mean reading it with a loved one in the room with you, or it might mean reading it in private with the door closed.

I hope it finds you wherever you're at, and know that you can always put it down. You can come back to it at a better time for you, or you can never come back to it at all.

# Introduction

This book will often hurt; it will make you angry and will hopefully make you feel. My hope is that this hurt, this anger and these feelings will move you to change the way we think and talk about surviving sexual violence. Sexual violence is a pandemic happening across all intersections of society. The fact is that nearly a quarter of women and over 4 per cent of men have been sexually assaulted, or have had attempts made. Many of you will know this fact of sexual violence through your own bodies, or perhaps through the bodies of your loved ones. The knowledge in this book should not be a shock, nor is it new – Angela Y. Davis recounted the same problems back in 1981: 'Appallingly few women can claim that they have not been victims, at one time in their lives, of either attempted or accomplished sexual attacks.'*

On a wider scale, people have finally started talking openly about this reality of sexual violence. Since the #MeToo and Time's Up movements that began in 2017, a cultural conversation has been ignited about the prevalence, immediate impact and long-term effects that sexual

---

* Angela Y. Davis, *Women, Race and Class* Penguin Classics, 3rd October 2019

violence has on people. Even more recently, after Sarah Everard's kidnap and murder in March 2021, women and people of other marginalised genders in the UK took to parks, streets and social media to decry the violence we live with every day. Such movements brought to the cultural foreground conversations about sexism, misogyny, consent and trauma. From the entertainment industry to governments, from India to the USA, people began to listen to the pain we have been living with for ever. There have been a vast array of think pieces, academic articles, short films, psychology journals and mindfulness practices to come out of this gradual revelation of sexual violations in the world. Yet, in the aftermath of the most recent sexual assault I was subjected to, I struggled to find centralised spaces where survivors themselves talked openly and honestly about what this world is like; about what it really *feels* like to be in a body that was once taken away from you. Some of this book will be social critique, some of it memoir, and some of it my own guttural sounds of the pain and injustice I have felt. I largely wrote all of this for myself – for the young girl who used to feel so alone, hopeless and scared. I am only in my mid-twenties, so I still have much to learn, but I hope the wisdom I have been simultaneously unfortunate to learn as a result of my experiences, and privileged enough to gain through my ongoing education and societal position, will also help others.

Back in 2010, I was a teenager first realising that I'd survived sexual abuse as a young child. I spent most of my evenings surfing Reddit and Tumblr, searching for any reliable or accessible resource that I could identify my experiences with. I would only find stale web pages that looked like they'd last been updated in 2006, or books written by psychotherapists in the 1990s. Then, when I was later sexually assaulted at the age of twenty, I came to the brutal realisation that there was so little I knew both before and during my process of reporting this assault to the police. There were so many questions I had, so many things I didn't understand about it all, and I'd been too scared to ask. I needed to speak on this strange culture we live in, the anger and pain it ignites in survivors and the radical (yet achievable) changes that need to take place for any real progress to be made.

This book will take a deep dive into the nuanced experiences I've had as a survivor living in our rape culture. Most of the themes in this book are both strikingly simple and impossibly complex at the same time. The vein throughout is one of holding multiple truths and multiple feelings at once; of allowing complicated and messy feelings towards huge topics. We do not live in a binary world. The topics I talk of will be hard, complicated, nuanced and confusing. That is OK; sit with the complexities that may arise. I oscillate between spectrums of our power and vulnerability; anger and forgiveness (or indeed non-forgiveness, as will later become apparent); sexuality and asexuality; beauty and disgust. It's an attempt to look at the root system of rape culture and a survivor's place within it. I am proud of my identity aspects as a survivor, as being disabled and queer. But I also have many contradicting thoughts about these aspects of my identity. Writing this book has helped me learn endlessly, so you'll read the growing pains of my coming to terms with such contradictions. I've learned through discussions with loved ones, through reading books and blogs, through impossible thoughts and feelings, through rage and anger, through knowing it's OK to change my mind. I've learned through all these things to ultimately realise that it's OK if we don't have a definitive answer for everything.

I struggled with the idea of splitting the pieces into chapters or sections – the nature of survival means everything is so intertwined. For ease and to allow people to dip in and out where they see fit, I have split the book into five sections and fourteen chapters. But know that, equally, all the parts could fit in any pattern; survival and healing are non-linear. I wrote this book in a way that means its parts and chapters can be dipped in and out of. The chapters can be read in isolation, skipped altogether or read chronologically. This was done for the purpose of accessibility. I don't want anyone who feels averse to certain topics to miss out on the book as a whole, and it's important to note that it's OK to read it however you see fit. There's also an index at the back of the book, so if you want to directly pick and choose what you read, please feel free to use this.

I need to make a few things clear at this point. I talk mostly on the reality of sexual violence perpetrated by cis men against women, but the things I talk about are by no means an exhaustive list of the lived realities of people across the world. Women are more likely to have experienced sexual violence, and cis men are more likely to perpetrate such violence, with 98 per cent of rape survivors in the last three years saying their attackers were male. I myself have only been victimised and survived violence by cis men. However, no single gender can claim victimhood, and none can be ascribed perpetrator status. Sexual violence is about the abuse of power, but currently our patriarchal societies mean that men are in power, and accordingly are in more of a position to abuse it over marginalised genders. Women and feminised bodies (i.e. people on the trans and non-binary spectrum, as well as cis men who are feminised in various ways, including their sexuality and gender expression) have to negotiate sexual violence in its various forms on a daily basis.

I feel I should also state, for full transparency, that there are still various restrictions over what I can and can't say, which is in itself typical of rape culture and the nature of abuse. I talk about the various abuses I've suffered throughout the book, but I am still gagged in various ways, both psychologically and legally, and thus certain deep truths have had to be avoided. I can't say absolutely everything I want to say. I can, assuredly, say more than I could when I made a podcast for a major broadcasting corporation, but until rape culture finally comes to its knees, there will always be limits. A large part of this gagging is for the purpose of protecting others; I fall into what Rebecca Solnit refers to as 'woman's learned help-fulness'. Maybe one day I will be able to say everything I want to say, claim everything I truly want to, but right now it's not reachable for me. Everything in this book, to my knowledge, is true. However, I have changed some names and places to protect myself and other people, or to avoid unnecessary legal hassle from perpetrators. The general story is the same, except for small details.

Another note that must be made is that, whilst I do use statistics throughout the chapters, statistics cannot provide the whole picture. While they're helpful to refer to and to give grounding to our arguments, most statistics only paint part of the picture, not the whole thing.

My words will often step out of line from the expected narrative of the perfect victim or good survivor. I am indeed normatively identified with many qualities of the perfect victim: I am white, middle class, perceived as cisgender and conventionally attractive. Yet, I hope my words rebel. I rebel with my words because I can, because I am seen as respectable by the wider world and have been given the privilege to use my voice. I want to use this voice to speak of the truths of our current realities and the defunctness of our current justice and support systems. Will this voice only be heard in an echo chamber? Perhaps, but it's worth shouting it all anyway.

Throughout the process of writing this book, my mental headspace was, for the most part, pretty good. I was stable, grounded, supported. I'm not always this levelled. We must keep in mind that not all survivors can keep such a straight face in the wake of violence. We are often deemed 'crazy', 'insane', 'nasty', 'bitches'. We are not always eloquent, and we shouldn't have to be for those in positions of power to sit down and try to understand what we're saying.

Too much time over the past few years has been spent focused on the perpetrators of sexual violence. We, as survivors, are left in the shadows, often protecting ourselves for the sake of anonymity or as a result of not wanting to be reduced to some of the most traumatic moments of our lives. I want to speak out, adding my voice to the cacophony of survivor's stories. But I also want to talk about things not often addressed in mainstream survivor circles. I want to talk about the chronic physical pain and illness many of us live with daily; the frequent suicidal ideations that appear throughout our lives; the way our vulvas can hurt for years after the violence takes place; how plainly devastating it is to have gone through such trauma; how abysmal the criminal justice system is at finding justice and the fact that abusers (despite what we often want to believe) are human too. It's not fluffy and it's not fun, but it's real. All of it is the way that I – and the way that we together – survive. I also hope to share some of the survivor skills I've had to develop over the years: openness, understanding, holding complexity, rage and empathy. Leah Lakshmi Piepzna-Samarasinha draws light to this fact that survivors gain direct skills from their survival. I am not this effective in conveying my feelings despite my survival, but indeed *because* of it. Survivors adapt and these adaptations can be genius.

This book should make you angry. I know that I am endlessly, relentlessly angry. From the intrusive police process to the cruel or thoughtless reactions society breeds in the people around us, to the lack of support we receive from various institutions that we thought would protect us – the information in this book will often hurt. But my hope is that it will also help you work with that anger to create change, both in yourself and in the world around you. Anger is important and it is necessary; it should not simply be scrubbed away or buried further inside you. Use the anger – channel it into activism, care work, community and art. Channel it into trying to change this hellscape for those who come after us. For there will be more after us, trying to survive in this painful place.

If you're a survivor, I hope that you may recognise parts of my story and outlook, and hopefully you may find some company. Survivorhood is a lonely and scary place at times, so if you're struggling to find the words or space to access your feelings, or if you just need to read someone who 'gets it', then I hope my words can be a small path to follow. I hope the company can make you just a little more comfortable in the discomfort of it all, if even for a moment. If you don't consider yourself a survivor, I hope that you'll be able to learn something from my embodied experience. Empathy, understanding and care is the only way I can see through all of this, so please do try to keep an open mind throughout. I question society and its norms through the lens of my own experience, that of surviving childhood sexual abuse and sexual assault in adulthood. The personal is always political, and this is my personal. Accordingly, I can only talk about these topics from my own embodied experience, but I will also try to shed light on the ways that other people can be and are affected by sexual violence and trauma. My experience is just one story, but the kernels of my story echo those of millions of survivors across the world.

# I

# Language and Definitions

# Chapter 1

# The Infinite Grey

What are we talking about when we talk about rape and sexual violence? Our views around this are inextricable from what we are told by institutions and what we are shown by the media. We have been told by the Sexual Offences Act 2003 that rape is the penetration of a vagina, mouth or anus by a man's penis (the pronoun 'he' is exclusively used in the documents). The act itself does not tell us this next part, but from the media and the world around us we can intuit that the rapist is a stranger, or near stranger, and the fragile woman victim will be innocent and at no fault – the perfect victim. Rape is still perceived as an act in which a strange, shadowy man drags a woman down a back alley at knifepoint. This perfect victim implies the existence of the imperfect one; the one who is to blame; the one who had it coming; the victim that so many of us are seen as.

The words that we use matter. That's why it was so painful for me to be told that what happened to me three years ago was 'sexual assault by penetration', as opposed to rape. The authorities, the police and the rape crisis centre insisted that this was 'just a legality', and that no hierarchy was being enforced upon my situation. So why did this hurt so much? Why does it still hurt so much? It makes me question whether I have the right to name my rapist a rapist. Do I have to refer to him each time as 'the man who assaulted me'? That's quite a mouthful. He *feels* like my rapist so that is how I choose to refer to him, no matter what the law regards him as. What that man did to me, and what other men had previously done to me, exists within the grey area of sexual violence.

So, what are these grey areas? The 'blurred lines', as a musician once sang in a long-forgotten song. Although the experience of stranger rape denoted above does indeed occur to a small number of victims – 15 per cent of women and almost half of male victims were assaulted by a stranger (Office for National Statistics, 2020) – the reality is that 90 per cent of victims know their abuser prior to the violence. In the year ending March 2020, it was found that more than half of women who had experienced rape or assault by penetration had been attacked by a partner or ex-partner, whilst 10 per cent had been by a family member. More than this brute fact, there are so many experiences that happen to us that we are unsure about, hesitant to label as assault or rape, because we are too scared and ashamed: scared to label ourselves with the purportedly pathetic brush of victimhood; ashamed to be seen as too weak. Scared to claim something that doesn't belong to us, to be seen as attention-seeking or overexaggerating. We shame ourselves, mirroring what society tells us, that what happened wasn't 'that bad', that we're making a big deal out of nothing. I have had multiples of these 'things' happen to me that fall into this grey area of trauma and violence. Perhaps I was too afraid to acknowledge it as assault out of a fear that yet another violation would have been made against me. The acknowledgement would have led me once more to ask the question, 'Why my body, why me?' I also would have been afraid that had I been 'found out', had I told someone about one of these elusive times, perhaps my other experiences of abuse would have become less legible. I would have cried rape too many times. Instead of chasing away the wolves that had done these things to me, I thought (or knew) I would have been left in the snow for more to come. I had already denied myself before I could speak those stories to anyone. So, I didn't let myself feel those abuses, didn't let myself process them. Some of these nights I speak of are only small holes at the back of my brain now. I can see them like a painting at the back of an attic, dust-covered with flecks of vividness. Maybe I will pull them out one day; or more likely, I will not.

When I talk of the events that shaped the course of my life, I employ varying degrees of honesty (and sometimes brutality) in the language I use. I talk about my extended and complicated family history in Ireland and the USA. I talk of my cherished childhood friendships and the way we made potions out of mud in my garden. I talk of my first love and its tumultuous (read: toxic) effects on my early adulthood. I talk of the people I've dated and the confusion they often leave me in. I talk of the biphobia I experience and the homophobic attacks I've been subjected to. I talk of having mental breakdowns, periods of hypomania, being suicidal, the effects of my

medication and related problems with substance abuse. I
talk of the everyday physical pain I live in. I talk of the
amount of emotional labour demanded of me in the work
that I do. It's pretty easy to be upfront about all that.

Talking about rape culture and survival is my job, so
you'd think I would automatically and proudly claim my
survival and the things that I've lived through. But lately,
I've begun doubting the unashamed confidence I thought
I had for my survival. I am deeply proud of myself for
my tenacity against these terrible things, but I began to
notice something about the cryptic language I use when
speaking on my survival. My language, both personally and
publicly, often falls short of the confidence I promote in
celebrating my survival. When I talk of my assaults, I find
myself avoiding the brutal facts. The norm when I talk of
the assaults usually follows the theme of: 'what happened
with (insert name)'; 'the *thing* that happened in (insert
place)'; 'what happened when I was travelling'; 'the *thing*
that happened in 2017'; 'the *thing* that happened when I
was young'; 'the childhood stuff'. I understand why I use
such elusive phrases with most people – I do not owe the
brutal truth to everyone I meet, no matter how much of
an oversharer I may be. But, even with those closest to
me, those who have helped me sift through excruciating
details and seen me cry – my best friends, my mum –
why can't I say, 'when I was sexually assaulted' or 'when
I was sexually abused' or the most dreaded of all: 'when
I was raped'? There are also those euphemisms used by
the wider world, the doubters, devil's advocates, neutral
press junkets; the legal jargon and gaslighting techniques.
For example, when a woman accused Donald Trump of

raping her (allegations he denies), her claims were reported as him having forced himself 'on' her, not 'in' her, as was the brutal reality of the accusation.

The real words hit me in my stomach, open me up as I try to say them more often in all the truth that they are. The words, the truth of what happened, sometimes become more muddied than the acts themselves, slick with the shame and guilt that society has taught us to feel as survivors of sexual violence. You worry it'll make you seem dramatic or 'crazy', that it'll make you seem too loud or too controversial. You worry it'll make the person you're talking to uncomfortable, and you *know* it will make you uncomfortable. But aren't we already uncomfortable? The silencing of the truth, the avoidance of reality, perpetuates the stigma that already falls so hard on survivors. This use of language is not a fault of us survivors – really, it's a strength; a way of protecting ourselves from the harshness of what the world thinks of us. We have to protect ourselves and we do so with euphemisms and brevities. We make things just that bit easier for ourselves by not having to voice the terrors of our pasts. We make the words lighter because we think it will stop them feeling so heavy.

We shouldn't have to use these devices to protect ourselves – we should already feel safe in speaking our truths. We should be supported by those around us in our society to speak our realities, and we should be allowed to use whichever words feel right in expressing ourselves. With the risk of being predictable here, let's compare the use of our language of rape culture to the usual honesty used with other crimes: 'when I was beaten up', 'when my house was broken into'. For these crimes, we don't use timid, cotton-wooled language. The crimes, though obviously very different in nature, still all consist of some person taking something from another; they all consist of a victim who was not to blame; they are all a form of violence. The language used when talking of sexual assault and rape extends the shame and guilt that survivors suffer. The hiding, the quietness of it all, makes us wonder: was it my fault? If I can't say it out loud, if I can't put it in the right words, maybe it wasn't that bad? If it just makes people feel awkward, perhaps I shouldn't bring it up, maybe I shouldn't speak of it at all?

The elusive language of survival can be comforting and is often nothing to do with protecting perpetrators. It is solely to do with protecting ourselves, and that is completely fine. The only thing that matters is that we have to do what is right for us and what feels best in the aftermath of our trauma; our own personal language, and whatever feels right and will best support us. This may mean switching your language around and trying out different terms for a while. Personally, I am going to start trying to reclaim the words of the terrible things people did to me to try and clear out the tough stains of shame and guilt. I am trying to say it more. So, I will write it: I was sexually assaulted, I was sexually abused, I was raped.

When I was about to begin recording my podcast, I had an existential crisis about how I would define myself in regard to my childhood sexual abuse. Sure, I am a survivor of sexual abuse, but there are certain other details and terms I can label myself with in relation to this (I am deliberately being elusive here). I felt so much guilt for not claiming these other terms, so much guilt for leaving those experiences further in the dark, shrouded once more in shame. I had a therapist at the time, a friendly woman called Melissa from New York. I spoke to her about this guilt, this burden of perpetuating shame. If I was calling myself such an activist, how could I still be hiding a part of my experience? Her surprisingly simple solution: you don't have to be an advocate for absolutely everything you've experienced. She told me it was OK to know my limits, to reserve a part of myself I am not yet ready to share with the entire world. This advice follows me now, a kind reminder in my ear when I start to spiral about my work. I didn't know that it was OK for me to protect myself in this sort of activist work. I thought I had to be endlessly, radically honest, to write my whole self on the page to exorcise the pain out of me in order to show others that they weren't alone and, in the vein of honesty here, to prove to others that I am qualified to hold this space as someone who has had it 'that bad'.

I find myself in a conundrum: is it better to be honest, by which I mean radically, completely, peeling-my-skin-off honest, or protected? Wouldn't it be more honest to admit to myself that I have boundaries, that I cannot be everything for everyone all the time? The type of childhood sexual abuse I survived is stigmatised. All childhood sexual abuse is stigmatised, but different kinds can be more or less so. I have struggled over my creative career in coming to terms with the fact that I can't label myself in certain honest ways because of personal reasons. Who gets the right to decide how I tell my story? I would like to say solely me: *I am a strong survivor and I reclaim my story.* But that isn't the truth. It isn't just my story to tell. I, along with everyone else on this planet, exist in a structure of relationships. I exist in various institutions: school, university, family, the state. Grace M. Cho, in reference to her work about the Korean diaspora after the Korean War that centres on her mother's own history with trauma and mental illness, discusses how some of her family members objected to her writing about her mother's personal history. Cho still decided to write the book with the honesty that some of her family could not accept. Is it her story to tell? In her case, I am not in a position to judge. In my own case, I am talking of my own personal history, but it's also a history that intrinsically involves other people. What is sexual violence but something that occurs between more than one person?

So, I wade between the two: sometimes honest beyond my bounds and sometimes protective of my stories. There are some things that are too hard to write and some things I am not supposed to say for the protection of others. There are some excruciating, life-shattering things that occurred as a side-effect of my abuse that I can't write about here. How do I come to peace with that? Is this anger I still have intrinsically tied to this enforced quietness on some matters in my personal life? And how do you write about something whilst not writing it, avoiding the actual words? Is it the in-between space that speaks?

Sexual violence is incredibly complex and strikingly simple at the same time. Sexual violence is the catcall we hear on the way to work when we take out our headphones for a moment. It is the fact I was spiked in a club when I was eighteen years old and brushed it off as a slightly scary anecdote to tell in the years following. It is the fact that almost all of the women and non-binary people I know have been sexually assaulted or abused in some capacity. It is the fact that all of them have definitely been sexually harassed. Sexual violence is the insidious monster of patriarchy and misogyny, concoctions of brutal power and cruelty. It's also the millions of stories we will never hear from individual victims and survivors within these systems of power and violence. Sexual violence is both the black and white and the infinite grey in between.

In workshops I teach where we talk about sexual violence and the ways in which we can help by intervening when we witness it, we discuss something called 'the continuum of sexual violence'. Liz Kelly coined this term in 1988 to propose that people's lived experiences of sexual harm can't be contained within legal parameters, for example those set in the Sexual Offences Act 2003. The continuum, distinct from a hierarchy, is comprised of an endless number of sexually violent behaviours. All of the behaviours contribute to the culture that enables some people to exercise power, control and violence over other people's bodies. All of the acts of harm I talk about within this book exist within this continuum, and each act is entwined with one another. When a rape joke is made or enabled, it makes room for leniency when other acts of sexual violence take place. Consider how far people take the idiom that it's 'just boys being boys' – we may hear it in a schoolyard one moment, then in regard to the United States' Supreme Court nomination in another. A rape joke that is laughed off, a proclaimed ignorance of groping in a nightclub or a belittling of a catcall makes room in our culture for 'worse' forms of sexual violence to be ignored too. When acts of violence are seen as 'not that bad', it ensures the continuation of the rape culture we live in. If someone jokes 'She was asking for it, though', a hollow space is carved out for sexual violence to be laughed at, lightened, excused.

Societally, different acts of sexual violence are indeed placed on a hierarchy, but there is no good to be found in placing one act of violence at a higher level of importance over another. Seeing a physically violent rape as 'worse' than being groped by an acquaintance in a bar does nothing but place some experiences in the shadows of silence. Both of these occurrences are acts of violence and both of these things need to be confronted and prevented, and the victims of both deserve community help. As Amy Dorris, actress, model and just one of the accusers of Donald Trump said when she accused Trump of forcefully kissing her: 'A violation is a violation.' Prioritising sexual violence that is 'worse' is also laced with various prejudices that we all hold. If we place acts of sexual violence on a hierarchy, we depend on forms of testimony and a belief that harms those whose lives and experiences exist on the margins. To prioritise a violent physical rape that has led to the prosecution of the rapist at the 'top end' of the scale relies on the defunct criminal justice system, ingrained beliefs about who is to be believed and in what ways, and the myth that visible physical violence is synonymous with 'true' rape. In her essay on female pain, Leslie Jamison says, 'Sure, some news is bigger news than other news. War is bigger news than a girl having mixed feelings about the way some guy slept with her and didn't call. But I don't believe in a finite economy of empathy; I happen to think that paying attention yields as much as it taxes.' We don't need to have limited empathy when we hear varying accounts of survivors' experiences of sexual violence – there is room for all of us on the continuum.

When dismissals are heard, we have to question whether an experience is being seen as 'not that bad' in comparison to another act of sexual violence, or whether it's being seen as not 'that bad' to begin with. Those who argue against the severity of an individual's experience of sexual violence tend not to be doing so in the selfless name of defending other survivor–victims. It's akin to when misogynists decry 'Men Too', only ever in response to a woman's declaration of sexual violence – all too often, these decriers are nowhere to be seen in places where male survivors actually need advocating for.

The ways we will react in the aftermath of experiencing sexual violence also exist in a vast grey area. Some people may recover quickly and will be satisfied with leaving the memory of abuse or assault behind them. Others will live their life alongside the abuse, circling around it, feeling its intensity to varying degrees over the years. Others may forget about it for years to come and remember it when they experience something similar, or they may remember it seemingly out of nowhere. Some survivors may be severely affected their whole lives by something that was deemed 'not that bad' by society. The infinite grey can manifest in an endless number of ways. If it happened when you were a child. If it happened yesterday. If it happened twenty years ago. If it happens next week. If you reported it to the police instantly. If you waited a year. If you went forward with your case. If you dropped the case. If the police let you down and sprinkled seeds of guilt in your mind. If the police helped you. If the police interrogated you in interviews. If you didn't go to the doctors. If you went to the doctors and they invalidated you. If you are on medication. If you are disabled (physically and/or mentally). If it was a friend. If you initiated the intimacy. If the court case was too much. If the abuser was found 'innocent' by the court. If they didn't get prosecuted. If they are still in your life. If you were drunk. If you were high. If you were young. If you were out late. If you walked home alone. If you were wearing a certain type of clothing. If you are queer. If you loved them. If you still love them. If you're a sex worker. If you can't remember everything. If you said yes at first. If you said yes later on. If you are involved in kink. If you're involved in BDSM. If no one believes you. If you don't believe yourself. If you have recovered. If you haven't confronted it. If you have had therapy. If you haven't had therapy. If you are angry. If you are so, incredibly, incomprehensibly angry. If you have forgiven your abuser. If you haven't forgiven your abuser. If you never want to forgive your abuser. If you have repressed it. If you know other people who have had 'worse' things happen to them. If it's 'something that happens to everyone'. If you have hurt people too. If you are trans. If you are a man. If you are a woman. If you are gender-non-conforming. If you had to do certain things to escape the attack. If you fought. If you ran away. If you froze. If you befriended your attacker. If you are not 'surviving'.

If you are all of the above, some of the above, none of the above: you are valid. Your survival is valid, and no one can tell you that you are experiencing your truth wrongly. You are the only one who can know what it's like in your body. We are not defined by what happened to us, but we are defined by the fact that we survive it – by the fact that we are still persisting despite it all.

The word 'trauma' literally translates from the Greek word for wound or injury. We can be traumatised by any number of things in our lifetimes: families, break-ups, grief, accidents, racism, bullying. In our modern common vernacular, however, 'trauma' tends to be equated with some form of violence or abuse, namely war and rape. Some trauma, as with wounds, can be healed; some can be partially healed, and some will never heal. Healing does not have to equate to finality, something I hadn't realised until I began the process of writing this book. Originally, this segment was a seething take-down of notions of healing within the survivor sphere. Journeys, scars, battles and healings crowded the vernacular I saw across social media and in literature about sexual violence. I worried that all these notions of healing suggested some sort of end-goal we must aspire to ultimately reach.

Healing, as it is commonly discussed, evokes an end-point of an idealised 'wellness', a cure for the craziness. Scars suggest the end of an injury, a cauterising of the hurt. My original qualm with narratives of healing was rooted in the woo-woo culture that can be found across so many discussions of being a survivor. Faux spirituality and memes would come to the fore, declaring that we're like butterflies erupting from our chrysalis of trauma, or that we're women warriors against the evil monsters who have harmed us. Buzzwords are used: journeys, honouring, manifesting. To me, these felt tiring. In my life, there will be no finality to the effects of trauma. As a survivor of both childhood sexual abuse and sexual assault in adulthood, the aftermath is both ever-present and ever-evolving. I will never reach the 'end' of my trauma. It will forever be a part of me, and that is not something to be ashamed of. The way that I survived what happened to me has helped to sculpt me at my very core.

In a talk you can find on Vimeo, Johanna Hedva talks on how the mark of trauma, and the continuation of your life despite it, may be better described as a callus rather than a scar. A scar implies the trauma doesn't hurt any more, that it's just a benign physical mark of something that tried to destroy you in the past. But our trauma often isn't as straightforward as that. It can be seemingly 'healed' for years, only to then come back, ripping out of our skin when we see someone who looks like our abuser on the bus or when we hear a song that transports us back to that evening we so wish to forget. More like a callus or corn, our past traumas can still exist as wounds on our skins, but they do not destroy us. We build up a resilience around them; we protect ourselves and become hard against all that has tried to destroy us. We grow around the mark, but it doesn't disappear, and it's still tender on certain days. We learn to live, and we learn to keep going with this hole we may now have. The callus may fall off and we may falter, wounds infected once more. But the callus will come back. Year after year, we will become resilient; we will keep going despite it all. And it is our own skin that has saved us, our own bodies that protect us from the trauma of what was done to us.

Throughout this book, a common theme will crop up: doubt. Or, more specifically, the experience of being doubted, silenced and dismissed, by the world, and by ourselves. When we go through sexual assault or rape, the trauma becomes twofold: there's the trauma itself, and then the trauma of being doubted. From having my experience doubted by people close to me, to being silenced and unofficially gagged by the criminal justice system and the harmful people they often protect, to medical professionals doubting my physical problems of pain and other 'mysterious' symptoms, to doubting my own memories and the physical pain I feel every day. My place within all of these experiences and systems has been murky and painted as a mystery that may or may not be solved. I survive within all of these over-lapping, ever-darkening grey areas: my childhood abuse was 'complicated', my most recent sexual assault was supposedly 'blurred lines', the untold ones are deemed by myself as 'not that bad', my physical health problems are still perceived as mysterious.

I sheepishly admit the superiority I can feel at the breadth of my abuses. Before beginning my website, podcast and now this book, I felt reassured in my position as a survivor as I had 'all my bases covered'. I had survived both childhood sexual abuse and multiple sexual assaults in my young adulthood. My cases aren't clear cut to society: I wasn't dragged down an alley, violently attacked or held down with extreme force. Yet, I have quantity, or, more aptly, consistency on my side. The person who abused me in my childhood acknowledged the abuse – had they not, perhaps my current story would look very different. A knock-on effect may have taken place and my latter assaults might have been dismissed too. I am caught in the double-bind that survivors must exist in: go through too much and you won't be believed (the girl who cried rape), go through too little and you won't be believed (it wasn't that bad). I find myself teetering on the edge, carefully trying to stay on the side of the believed. I find perverse confidence in surviving childhood sexual abuse; no one can believably tell me it was my fault – I was six years old. What a terrifying world to exist in, when I can only feel assuredness in the abuse that occurred when I was a six-year-old child.

I place myself at risk of witness reliability by admitting the confusion and incoherence I often feel about the violence I have survived. One day, I will believe myself wholeheartedly, proudly designating myself as a survivor once again. Another day, I will feel a fraud, particularly in the case of my most recent assault; that I aggrandised what happened. Were that case to go to court, such words and honesties would bring me to the door of the lying, perhaps not a false accusation but certainly an unreliable primary witness. By writing these very words, I give up my right to formal justice because I don't care for it now anyway. There exists within me two people – one who believes myself and wholeheartedly knows that the bad things that happened were *that bad*; and one who gets stuck in the wound of doubt, returns and tells me that it wasn't that bad, that I need to get over it. This latter self is one who's been moulded by past abusers, enablers and institutions. The fact that she's been moulded by such powerful voices makes her all the harder to ignore.

When I tell people directly of my experience as a survivor of sexual abuse and assault, or when someone sees the work I have done in which I voice my experiences and share others' stories with the world, I often am told that I am 'so brave'. Now, don't get me wrong, these people are well meaning. They see these words as affirming, kind and true. Yet, to me, they feel heavy; scripted and stabbing. This is what people think they're supposed to say to someone who has been through pain. I'm a hero, an inspiration.

But am I such a hero? What of my experiences, of what some men did to me, makes me a hero? Is it that I continued moving, continued living, despite it all? Was there supposed to be another option? What if I wasn't 'surviving'? What if I hadn't chosen to turn my pain into activism, didn't become some sort of survivor superhero? Some people never see themselves as having 'survived' and prefer to acknowledge themselves as victims of a crime – do they qualify as brave too? What about those who keep their abuse secret for their entire lives – do they qualify? Is there some sort of scale of braveness: how bad the assault was? How young you were when it happened? How people treated you afterwards? How I have capitalised on my pain to make some sort of silver lining out of the torture?

The speakers of such phrases are not being cruel or pitying. They say what they think they should because what else is there to say? The conversations about survival and coping are so limited in our societies, so of course people are left clueless over how best to respond. Another common response when one opens up to others about what they've been through is, 'I don't know how you do it'; 'I don't know if I'd be able to live with that'. To say these things to those who've experienced sexual violence is essentially telling us that they would rather be dead, rather be anything, than to be us, to have lived through the things that have occurred in our lives. It tells the survivor that they are now defined by their struggle. The declaration of bravery also tells us, as Alok Vaid Menon writes on the topic of calling people in the trans community 'brave', that the onus is on us as individuals to be brave, to stay tenacious and resilient in the face of oppression. At the end of the piece, Alok sums it up perfectly – 'They keep calling me brave, but I would rather be safe than that.'

Braveness also brings with it the fallacy of the perfect victim and the good survivor. Would I still be brave if I was seen as having been at fault in some way? Would I be seen as brave if I wasn't operating at my high-functioning, good-survivor level? I mentioned the 'perfect victim' in the opening of this chapter. By this, I mean the one who is portrayed to us throughout our society. It's the mythical victim we subconsciously expect to see – she will be sober, and she will be pure, she will be white, straight, cisgendered, sane and able-bodied. When you are declared a victim, you are always compared to this perfect ideal. You find yourself checking your alignment with them. When I was last assaulted, I was sober, I was wearing pyjamas. I had some things on my side. Other things weren't on my side – I had invited him over, it had initially been consensual. You find yourself questioning yourself like a defence lawyer.

I do not think I'm brave. I think I'm resilient and that I'm worthy of pride in myself and of the pride held by those who care for me. To me, being brave is when you take something upon yourself that you have chosen – standing up for an injustice that has happened to someone else, for example, or running into a hurricane or burning building to save a baby, something clichéd like that. I had nothing to do with what other people did to me; I had no choice. I was not accountable, and therefore I see no medal of 'bravery' in my survival. I see just that: my survival, my strength. I am not fearless and should not need to be. I think of myself and other survivors as so much more than all those things that the word 'brave' brings with it. We are resilient, even if we may not always feel it, and we are more than the all-too-often empty words of bravery that strangers may label us with. Even on the worst days, we persist against what has tried to pull us down. So, we don't have to be brave, we just have to *be*.

# Chapter 2

# What Rape Isn't
## (though sometimes it is)

Rape isn't poetic. It isn't a metaphor. Yet sometimes, I find memories of a specific assault seep into my psyche as a brutal poem, a beautiful nightmare. Maybe it's the writer in me. The assault I speak of was not the first, and it was not the last. It is the assault I actually talk least about, both in my personal relationships and in the work I have done. It is the one I carry most shame for, yet moments of that day still manage to fight their way through that thicket of shame. Nathan Shara writes in *Beyond Survival*, 'Shame creates an identity: "I am bad." Shame keeps us stuck, isolated, and hiding.' This shame is written into my DNA. I know all the right words to say about my experiences: that I ought not to be ashamed, that it wasn't my fault; that it is his shame, not mine. But it is harder to believe it, to truly feel it within myself. Maybe if I say it enough times it will become true.

I saw a whale that day. It should be a perfect memory, golden and encased in the Australian sun, the first whale I'd ever seen so close in real life. I stood on the shore-line of a deserted cove. The whale was about 400 metres offshore. It was so close, I thought it might have been a small shark at first. Then I saw the dark curve of it glide through the shallow waves, the small dorsal fin drifting, too long and stout to be a shark, too large to be a dolphin. It was a humpback whale, so close I might have been able to reach it in a matter of minutes had I dived into the Pacific Ocean. I didn't dive in as it was too cold; wintertime in Australia. Wintertime in July – a concept perhaps not completely alien to me as someone who grew up in the north-west of England. I watched the whale from the shoreline and, as quickly as it had come into my vision, it had gone, returned to the depths. I returned to my towel lying further up the beach. I lay in the still-warm sun and covered my bikini-clad body with another towel to keep in the warmth.

I was at the beach with a man. I can't remember where he was during my whale sighting. Was he beside me? I am certain he wasn't, but maybe I have erased him from this brief moment of joy. I think he was somewhere in the bush behind the beach, searching for something. I was staying with this man temporarily, as I travelled along the eastern coast of Australia in 2015. On that Sunday, he suggested that I could drive down with him for a couple of hours to this deserted beach where he wanted to surf. I was eighteen years old and trying to grasp any part of myself I had so desperately lost through a mental breakdown six months before. He assaulted me on that beach whilst I lay in the sun. I lay still, frozen and silent whilst it happened. He sexually assaulted me. I was wordless; empty. I couldn't move and I couldn't protect myself, and I felt that my body had betrayed me to this person's ugly violation of me.

There are so many things I admonish my eighteen-year-old self for when I look back on that day. I know others would have admonished me, would still admonish me, for them too. That's why I didn't tell anyone at the time. It's why I only told one friend some months later. This assault was not like the other two instances of sexual violence that had happened in my life before; I believed it would not be met with the same uncomfortable sympathy. I taught myself, through the lessons of society, that the experience should lead to shame, anger, disgust. These feelings have not left me – I still keep this incident shrouded in shame and secrecy. I still cut off its oxygen supply when it comes to me in my throat.

The things I admonish myself for: he was a stranger. I had known him for two days and had met him through a well-known travelling app. I got in a car alone with him and travelled to a deserted beach I had never been to before. I had already got a bad feeling around him and he had already been pushing my boundaries. I didn't say no when he started performing oral sex on me, I didn't push him away – I froze. I had an orgasm. I still hate my body so much for that, for betraying me.

These are all the things I need to write and say in response to those admonishments: I was eighteen years old. He, I believe, was in his fifties – something he had actively lied about. He seemed to prey on young and naïve women. I was eighteen, alone, traumatised (I had been raped two months before and was still very much at the beginning of my comprehension of my childhood abuse). I was *eighteen*. A teenager. A teenager who was sexually assaulted by a predatory man. My response was to freeze – freezing is one of the body's multiple forms of response to threat. I was asleep, he walked up to me from the shoreline, where the whale had been just moments before. He placed my shorts over my eyes so I could not see, and he violated my body. I could not move; I could not speak. But I came, so did I enjoy it? No, I did not enjoy it. My body reacted in a way I couldn't control, and I was trapped. I may still feel somewhat betrayed by my body, but I know it didn't mean to hurt me. It didn't ask for that to happen. *I* didn't ask for that to happen. It makes me feel sick to think of this assault, makes me feel dirty, like it was my fault and I had consented to sex with this harmful man. But I didn't. I was alone and scared, and he chose to take advantage of me. *He* chose to hurt me.

Rape isn't sentimental. But, on days like today, every second becomes steeped with the memory of three years ago. I remember a vast number of dates and times, places and sounds, each etched to important moments in my life. Did part of this blessed and cursed ability for memory come from my childhood abuse? Did it come from unleashing the past – a pathway uncovered and forever replicated with any significant moment I experience? Today marks three years since my most recent assault, the catalyst of all this outpouring. Three years ago, I was sick, I had a cold, and I asked the man I was seeing to come and bring me some tea at my home. The day itself, before he arrived was lovely. I remember I went to a Polish deli with my best friend and got pierogi and cannolis. We ate them in the park. It was the first days of spring. He met me later that evening at my nearest tube stop. We went to my home, and many things happened. He did many things that harmed me.

Lots of things have happened in those three years. I have started my career in creative activism against sexual violence. I have fallen in love. I have made new friends and fallen in platonic love over and over again with my long-time friends. I finished my undergraduate degree and my master's. I have travelled to different countries. I've had great sex and found someone who has made me feel like I deserve pleasure. Yet, on days like today, when the memories begin to break the riverbanks of my mind, it becomes hard to feel my body in the present.

For those who haven't been sexually assaulted or abused, or those who don't recount or pay attention to the anniversary of the dates of such things, it can be analogised to an anniversary of the death of a loved one. It is the anniversary of the death of a part of me that I will never get back. There is a reason why the memory of this specific assault is so etched into my psyche. I cannot remember the date of the other three major assaults off the top of my head. I know the season my childhood one occurred in. I know the months of the other two. But I know that the most recent assault occurred on a specific day during a specific month of a specific year. I know this because I wrote about the assault in my journal the morning after it happened. Eight months later, I had to transcribe this diary account into a note I would take in with me to my initial police meeting, before I would officially report it. They took this account from me, a paragraph printed on an A4 piece of paper, even though I had recounted it to them in this consultation and they had written it all down. A week or two after that, I had to tell them what happened again, this time in a police interview room. I had to state the date again and again and again. Perhaps one day the pointed pain of the day will fade; perhaps I will only remember a few days after the day has passed, then a few weeks, and then not at all. Perhaps, but not this year. This year I remember just as urgently as the morning after.

Rape isn't linear. Lidia Yuknavitch says on memory, 'Events don't have cause and effect relationships the way you wish they did. It's all a series of fragments and repetitions and pattern formations . . . All the events of my life swim in and out between each other. Without chronology. Like in dreams.' I perhaps narrate my trauma chronologically – as I do often throughout this book, as social norm dictates. Many of us tell our stories this way, but that's not really how they come to me. If I am mapping out my history, I can mould my experiences with sexual violence and trauma into a neat chronology.

In the everyday, they come to me as a flood, over-whelming and messy, filled with debris. A memory from one night a few years ago may come soaked in the deluge with a memory from when I was six years old. The years apart become milliseconds. I always have the capacity to swim or to drown. That night three years ago comes to me in flashes, and with these flashes, or drips, comes the lightning storm, or the flood. The way he held me down when I was twenty brings with it the smell of that bathroom when I was six. The words he said flow in with the pain that another man stabbed inside of me two years before that. The bodily memory of frozen limbs and numb lips are stitched with the tight shutting of my eyes. Their faces pour into my mind, along with their hands and the words they plastered in my ears. It's like I can't let one of them in without them all tagging along. My body protects me in these moments, keeps me afloat by letting me drown. I shut down and shake, unable to resurface for what could be minutes or hours. When I return to reality and full consciousness, the storm has passed.

Now, three years after the assault, my triggers and panics have significantly subsided. They may return with cataclysmic force, but for now I feel calmer. I still think of him, still get the incessant urge to check his social-media account to 'keep tabs' on where he is. I used to kid myself that this checking, which I used to do like clockwork once a week, was for my own protection. I know now that it was a trauma response. It was a subtle form of self-harm, reminding myself of the pain and the panic I tell myself I should be feeling to stay safe. This year, I blocked him on social media, a big step in preventing me from obsessively practising this ritual. The intense grief of survival slowly turns into the everyday.

Rape is subjective. I recently came to the realisation that no one truly knows what I've lived through. That may seem a truism to many, that only you can ever really know your own experiences, but I have had cognitive dissonance over this idea for as long as I can remember. I assume others, especially those closest to me, know things about me that they would have no way of knowing. I once told my partner the abridged version of one of my assaults, a story that's only been entirely (painstakingly) heard before by detectives when I gave them my official statement. I left out the horrific details for him: the words said to me, the way I cried and squirmed, the way I lay stiff in the throes of panic. I've realised that I talk objectively about my trauma, my survival, my assaults and rapes, but I never go further. I never truly allow others into the terrors that those men have subjected my body to.

I carry the archive of memories in my mind, a glimpse of his hands here, the blindfolding of my eyes there, the smell of the linoleum floor in the bathroom. I see the face of David (the pseudonym I give to one of the men who assaulted me) as I walk to get the tube; I hear people talking about Airbnb and I'm taken back to that man's dirty body; people joke about things that remind me of the shame I have lived in since I was a child. As I've already said, these memories are never chronological, never coherent. They come from years apart, but all the hands that have violated me mould into one giant fist, crushing my mind of all sense of safety and reality. It comes quicker and clearer when my mind is at its weakest. I want to paint it all on a mural, I want to carve it into my front door, I want to make it into a feature-length film. Then other people would have to endure what goes through my mind on repeat.

I told my partner that I had assumed he already knew everything, but now I realise that this is only because it plays out in my own mind so often that I'd forgotten he couldn't see it too. It played behind my eyes so regularly that I thought I had somehow projected the scenes onto the walls of the people I love. Surely they can see the pain too? I get angry, I cry, I become distant because I assume that they should have seen what happened to me. The reality is that I rarely explain what actually happened.

I know I shouldn't have to explain myself to be believed, but it's as though I want to, need to. I need people to believe me in order to believe myself; to know that I'm not exaggerating, that I'm not a fraud, that my whole life hasn't been based on something that wasn't even 'that bad'. I know I need to find solace within myself, that all I need to find comfort in is what I know to be true and real about my life. But the truth is that I need to be reassured, I need to be held and to be reminded that what they all did to me was wrong, that I'm not crazy and that I deserve to be safe. I need to know that I will forever be safe from the kinds of harms perpetrated by those men in the past, even when that promise may not necessarily be true.

I can't say these words out loud. These words originally came in the form of a letter to my partner, trying to explain my anger and upset at his lack of clarity around my experience. It is much easier to type these words, the page a buffer from really having to say them. It twists my stomach that the only words I can ever think of for my assaults are words usually reserved for consensual intimacy. So, I'm going to try and find other language here. It wasn't licking or fingering, it was stabbing. It wasn't love, it was violence. It wasn't sex, it was rape. I still don't feel worthy of that final word, my conceptions and values in my own experiences diminished in the darkness of what the law and the world tell me is 'bad enough'.

I say all the right things and I know all the right words to say to other people, but deep within myself I still feel ashamed and deeply insecure – that I was crazy, that they were right and that I am wrong. My own mind becomes a judge, a jury. My worst enemies are in my head, taunting me, laughing at me as they scream in my ears that I'm a fraud, a fraud, a fraud. It wasn't that bad.

But it was that bad. It was always that bad. I am all the proof you need.

# Chapter 3

# Kiss Chase

At five years old, in infant school, we played a game called 'kiss chase'. The game consists of one team chasing the other around, and if one player tags another they get to kiss them. The teams were sorted by gender – boys and girls. During one specific game of kiss chase, it was 'boys on girls' (the patriarchy really does start young). A boy chased me (a boy who I believe turned out to be a perfectly pleasant man, I should clarify) and he 'tagged' me. Upon the tagging, he slipped, and pushed me headfirst into a fence. My face was smashed, and I got a nosebleed. It was a cruel introduction to the world of courtship and pursuing intimacy. It may have been a silly children's game back then, but it's hard to ignore the stark metaphor of culturally ingrained misogyny.

Fast forward a decade. At fourteen, on my way home from school in my uniform, a friend and I were catcalled on my road. The group of builders shouted something – I'm not sure what – and we smiled, laughed along with them. In the same year, a small group of girl-friends and I were 'flashed' by a man on a back street of Manchester's Northern Quarter one Saturday afternoon.

Perhaps 'flashed' is too delicate a word: he pulled down his trousers and showed us his penis, holding it towards us. He laughed, and so did we. We squealed as over-whelmed teenagers do. Our young minds couldn't process the stark violence that had just occurred. Two years later, at sixteen, on my lunch break during my first day of sixth form, I was catcalled by another group of builders in my hometown centre. I'd picked that outfit for the first day so carefully and was so pleased with my newfound fashion. The attention paid to me instantly turned my pride to embarrassment – obviously my skirt must be too short. I didn't wear another skirt for a few weeks after that - I'd realised trousers were safer. Through these moments (and countless others), I was taught what every young woman is – that our bodies aren't just our own. We're perceived as existing for the purpose of the male gaze, especially when we're in public.

All women, along with other marginalised genders, are familiar with what Caren Beilin refers to in *Blackfishing the IUD*, as 'basket men': they stand on the street and collect your image, 'being baskets for female fear . . . They are collecting, with their eyes, control . . . to watch is powerful enough . . . is to say "I could do more," is to spread horrific mercy into the atmosphere.' These basket men, the creeps who leer at us as we walk about our days, are persistent pieces of furniture in our rape culture. The staring and leering, a form of sexual harass-ment according to the UK Equality Act 2010, persists throughout the year, especially in cities and populated towns. In London, my city of the past half a decade, sexual harassment becomes a daily expectation. Whoever invented earphones has become one of my most favoured feminist allies, for the number of times I have blocked out harassment by blasting music through them. I happily choose an increased likelihood of hearing damage over having to hear harassment most days.

Street harassment of young women and girls (colloquially known in English-speaking countries as catcalling) is highly prevalent in the UK, with a report by UN Women UK in 2021 finding that 97 per cent of women aged 18–24 said they'd been sexually harassed, whilst 80 per cent of women of all ages said they'd experienced sexual harassment in public spaces. Catcalling happens across society, especially impacting those deemed feminine (women, non-binary people and gay men), those who are vulnerable to racist attacks and those across the LGBTQ+ spectrum. The act exists on the continuum of sexual violence, but to wider society's eyes it's often seen as 'not that bad'. In turn, we brush off our own experiences of this violence. Amongst the 1,000 women surveyed for the UN Women UK survey, 96 per cent didn't report their experience of harassment, with many thinking the incidents – including groping and stalking – weren't serious enough to report. We go to the shops, we're harassed; we get on the tube or the bus, we're harassed; we walk to the park, we're harassed. And then we just have to continue on with our days afterwards.

What used to upset and anger me most about these catcalls, sometimes even more than the vulgar men themselves, was my own reaction. My response would be to smile, having been socialised from such a young age to be pleasant and kind to strangers, even if someone shouted something at me, even if it was full of vulgarities. Would I smile out of habit, awkwardness or fear? It's likely that it was all three of these reasons combined, alchemising into female subjugation.

One day during the first Covid-19 lockdown, while I was living at my partner's flat and he couldn't make it to the shops with me. I groaned in anticipation, knowing that when I walk around outside without him, I am harassed. I'm all for being strong and not needing a man for protection, but sometimes it just feels like a little bit too much of an effort. I was wearing shorts but decided I would change into yoga pants to try to avoid catcalls as best possible. My (cis, male) partner was tentatively appalled – was I really that at risk of harassment on a ten-minute walk to the Co-op? I smiled and rolled my eyes at his sweet naïvety. Lo and behold, minutes later on my solo walk, a black car started following me. I was listening to Rina Sawayama 'STFU' at full blast (quite appropriately) and caught the car out of the corner of my eye. The man driving was beckoning towards me. I took my headphones off, as is my knee-jerk reaction when someone first tries to get my attention, and quickly realised the danger of the situation. I put my headphones back in and started walking faster, breaking a sweat on the late-spring day.

The heat specifically seems to bring out the creeps. Although, of course, not exclusively; I've been catcalled whilst in a hat, scarf and winter coat. Back to the quick trip to the shops. The man in the car continued to follow me, and then decided to leave me alone. Minutes later, a group of teenage boys catcalled me, whistling and saying things I muffled out with my music. The socially distanced queue outside the Co-op looked on in pity, half smiling in their awkwardness at my sexual harassment in broad daylight. I returned home to my partner, almost gloating with how right my predictions had been.

So, why do men catcall us? The common response, if you've ever had enough energy to bother to confront a catcaller, runs along the lines of 'it's a compliment' or 'cheer up, love'. It could be possible they believe this is an effective strategy in flirting with someone you fancy, but this stance is plainly incorrect. In her book *Wordslut,* the feminist socio-linguist Amanda Montell outlines the way that catcalling goes against every norm of compliment behaviour that experts have studied. Montell also recounts an episode of the podcast *This American Life* in which journalist Eleanor Gordon-Smith took on the challenge of interviewing men who catcalled her on a busy street in Sydney. Only one man agreed to debate Gordon-Smith on the topic of catcalling, and despite her recounting numerous statistics and emotional stories in a two-hour-long conversation, this one man still refused to stop catcalling. Even when we do attempt to explain to men who are inclined to harass women how bad it is, they don't (and won't) stop.

This brings us to why men really catcall: power. Men on the street, or anywhere, who decide to harass someone else do so because they see the other person as an object. Montell names such behaviour 'a display of social control, signalling to women that they are intruders in a world owned by men, and thus have no right to privacy'. A man catcalling a woman implies that her looks and her sexuality are her most defining feature, and the fact he can call attention to that in the public realm shows her that he has the power to name it, and thus has power over her.

The catcalling man may also enact such behaviour to reaffirm to the world their own raw heterosexuality, and thus their corresponding power in our straight world. The power over others these macho men feel is interlaced with another trait: a lack of empathy. As Montell explains, if a victim confronts a catcaller, the catcalling man will often decry their own innocence, stating that their intentions were misconstrued. And this is the problem – they convince *themselves* that they're not to blame; that the victim is 'taking it too seriously', because they can only relate to their own humanity and not the lived experiences of the people they harass. They do this to uphold their own toxic masculine façade; empathizing with the feminine position places them in grave danger of becoming the feminine 'other' themselves.

I will admit that some days I'm a 'bad' feminist. I go outside knowing I look good: I'm having a good hair day; I'm wearing an incredible outfit and it's a rare day of wearing make-up. I'm catcalled, whistled at, called 'gorgeous' and I think 'I *know*, thank you!', my confidence reinforced. I was in my parent's garden one evening a few years ago. As I brushed dried grass off the back of my shorts, I grazed my butt with my curved hand in the process. I could hear workmen in the house next door, but they were shielded from view by trees. I thought to myself, 'If they could see me doing this, they'd be jealous

I get to touch myself here.' This thought came naturally. What began as a mindless action led to my own self-objectification, an action that reminded me those faceless men would likely see me as an object, an action that told myself to keep in line, to stay scared. I was my *own* basket man; I was the creep staring back at me. I saw myself, who loves my body and the curves and moles it holds, as a body that only exists for the eyes of the men we can always hear but can't always see. As men objectify us, we too can end up objectifying ourselves. I'd linked my self-worth to my sexual attractiveness for so long, I was only surprised by my reaction as an afterthought. We quickly grow out of our young girlhood and into the young women who view themselves as this gaze does.

This tendency develops early, and at fourteen, my friends and I realised we were finally wanted, perhaps even *needed* by the boy-men. There were over-padded bras and way too much make-up. I say this not because make-up is a bad thing generally, but because we were literally just wearing too much make-up – I'm talking clumped mascara, thick kohl eyeliner and Maybelline's Dream Matte Mousse foundation. My girlfriends and I had all previously been shy and awkward, thus unattractive to the 'cool' boys in our year, so when we started getting the attention of some boys in the year above, we jumped at the chance to hang out with them, drinking whatever we could find in our parents' alcohol cupboards in small suburban parks. My drink of choice was my parent's long-forgotten-about sherry mixed with Red Bull (which incidentally tastes like soy sauce, and was, as you might expect, extremely disgusting). I drank it down because I wanted to be fun, to be cool and desired. To be slightly out of your mind and body in the realm of silly drunkenness felt new, exciting, numbing. These boys we drank with were not particularly malicious, they were just stupid teenage boys, trying to have sex. None of us had been taught properly how to respect each other, and this lack of respect always came down harder on us girls.

This time period was exactly when I started to gain any ounce of confidence in myself. It was also when many great contradictions began, many of which remain; I became confident but also devastatingly self-conscious, constantly worried about what boys would think of me; I contemplated whether I was the 'ugly' one out of my friends, whether I could ever be 'chosen' by anyone; the desperation to lose my 'virginity' and be seen as worthy of love.

Through our socialisation and the representations of ideal femininity surrounding us in the media, these internal contradictions are solidified. This vicious cycle of love and hate for oneself still plays out as a tumultuous affair does on a soap opera. I love myself, but I also hate myself. I am inside myself, but always outside myself too. I know I am strong, but I also know I am too weak for the words of bravery people have sewn onto me. I know what is right in this world and what fights need to be fought, but I can't always see what is right for myself and that I need to fight for myself. I think I'm incredible, and I also think I'm a piece of shit. I know I am worthy, but I also know I am worthless. I notice all this, see the tides of lightness and heaviness pulling and pushing; loving and hating as summer and winter meld into each other. When does one end and the other begin? My answer is never, and each extreme of loving and hating, caring and cruelty, is inextricably intertwined, necessarily existing for the other to come along and wind itself into the mess of threads we call ourselves. Is this in the nature of the female condition or the survivor's condition?

When I started having sex with my first boyfriend, I wouldn't take my bra off for the first year because I was so embarrassed of my own naked body. I still feel these hangovers of teenage shame now; I feel awkward if my partner looks at me whilst I'm in a certain position or if the dress I bought is just a bit too transparent or short.

I don't remember these first sexual experiences as a time of sexual empowerment. It was always about the boy's pleasure; always about what he thought, what he wanted. We are told this, of course, through the society around us and the porn most popular within it. It's not that I wasn't sexual at this age – I had been sexual from a young age. I started masturbating when I was very young, humping pillows and rolled-up jumpers whilst imagining girls kissing. When YouTube came around and I got my hands on an iPod Touch, this imagining graduated into searching for 'girls kissing' on YouTube: *The L Word* best bits and *Sugar Rush* clips being my favourite pastimes (and I didn't come to realise I was bisexual until I was nineteen? Seems suspicious).

We weren't taught in our sex-education classes that sex was supposed to be about mutual pleasure. We weren't taught extensively about the nuances of consent – about the way it needs to be active, ongoing and enthusiastic.

About the way consent can be retracted at a later stage and that it needs to be freely given. We may have been loosely told that 'no means no', but no further exploration was attempted into the way that boys and men need to actively ensure consent; how they need to listen to 'no' and to be looking out for an uncomfortable 'yes'. Upon conducting my own informal research into the matter, an Instagram poll of my followers who attended school in the UK in the 2000s and 2010s found that 96 per cent of them hadn't been taught about consent.

I have two memories of sex-ed in my school. The first included purple dildos brought around by the French teacher. We were learning to put condoms on these dildos and the vulgar teenage boys in my class took it as an opportunity to slut-shame a girl in our class. It was an enlightening experience, at least into slut-shaming. One point for male-centred sexual health education, devoid of any female pleasure. The second memory is almost too ridiculous; I had to confirm with my old school-mates that this really did happen. I tried to google it, but obviously a load of porn just came up. The *A-Z of Sex* was a sex-education video consisting of Red Bull-style animated cartoons of an anthology of sex terms. The one I remember most was the cartoon for 'M'. You guessed it – masturbation. It consisted of a cartoon woman in her bath realising that she could use her shower head to masturbate with. To be fair to this cartoon, at least it showed a woman pleasuring herself. As you can imagine, a group of fifteen-year-olds could hardly handle this, and it was the raucous talk of our year for the rest of the day, calcifying shame for any girl who happened to relax by doing the very same thing. Thankfully, we did have one citizenship skills class from an LGBT community group (the Q+ wasn't added on). However, this centred solely around queer identities without addressing any sexual aspects. Of course, education about queer identity is vital, but it reminds us that we haven't come *that* far after the revoking of Section 28, a law prohibiting 'promoting homosexuality' in schools (and as result, effectively banning any mention of LGBTQ+ identity). My sex-education classes were only taking place a few years after Section 28 was finally revoked, after extensive campaigning from queer-rights groups, in 2003.

The sexual education of noughties Britain was always black and white, and always male-centric. We weren't taught at length about mutual pleasure, about active and ongoing consent, about the confusion around consent when it involves alcohol. If we'd have been taught about these things, would we have been better equipped to deal with our burgeoning sexualities? What if, alongside sexual education and healthy sex, we were also taught about sexual violence and abuse, taught about how to fight rape culture and unlearn toxic masculinity that had been bred within them from a young age? And what if we taught children and teenagers how to support their friends if they disclose sexual abuse to them?

As well as general healthy education about young sexuality, teaching young people about sex also acts as a safeguard against violence children may be subjected to. My Instagram poll found that 97 per cent of people in the UK in the 2000s and 2010s hadn't been educated about what to do if they were sexually harmed or abused. If we teach children the things they should see as wrong – being asked to do things they don't want to, being told to keep an adult's 'secret' – perhaps we could empower them to speak out about abuse at the time it occurs. If they were empowered to do so, active abuse could be stopped in its tracks, and healing from the abuse could begin years earlier for the victims, improving their chances of recovery and avoidance of life-altering conditions like complex post-traumatic stress disorder.

Nowadays, some progress has been made. Despite protests from some parents concerning the mandatory elements of relationships education for primary-school-aged children, including whether it should include the reality of LGBTQ+ relationships, sexual education in school has still relatively improved over the past decade. Although general sex education still isn't mandatory in the curriculum, according to the Department for Education, as a part of the mandatory Personal, Social and Health Education (PSHE), in Relationships Education (RSE) 'schools should teach pupils the knowledge they need to recognise and to report abuse, including emotional, physical and sexual abuse. In primary schools, this can be delivered by focusing on boundaries and privacy, ensuring young people understand that they have rights over their own bodies . . . Pupils should know how to report concerns and seek advice when they suspect or know that something is wrong.' In secondary school, sexual education is mandatory. This education includes being informed of different types of relationships, safety online, intricacies of consent and reproductive rights for people who can become pregnant. However, it seems that the actual education being delivered is done so on a postcode lottery. In 2016, the Sex Education Forum found that half of the young people they surveyed didn't learn how to get help if they were abused, over four in ten hadn't learned about healthy or abusive types of relationships, and 34 per cent hadn't learned about consent. What is needed to change these statistics? Another revamping of the curriculum? Better training for teachers? A report in 2018 by Barnardo's found a potential solution to this knowledge gap: young people are more comfortable talking to external facilitators about matters of sex and relationships, and plenty of groups exist to provide such education, groups like Big Talk Education and Split Banana, who deliver age-appropriate holistic sex education across the UK.

There are also other ways for young people (and adults alike) to learn productively outside of the formal classroom. Since the rise of YouTube and podcasts, technology has facilitated a democratic sexual education that has helped many young people become confident in their new sexualities whilst learning about complex subjects like consent and abuse. Projects have been established by duos like Come Curious, comprised of Amber Reed and Florence Bark, who have over almost 200,000 subscribers on YouTube and 1.5 million listeners to their sex-education podcast *F\*\*cks Given*, and who openly discuss sex to 'spread valuable knowledge and relieve some anxieties that surround the subject'; and the pair behind *Brown Girls Do It Too*, in which hosts Poppy Jay and Rubina Pabani chat with a guest about their sex lives as South Asian women. Sex education is also provided by individuals, such as Jimanekia Eborn, a sex educator and trauma specialist who hosts *Trauma Queen*, a podcast series in conversation with other professionals and non-professionals about sexual trauma and its intersections with race, disability and sexuality. There are other individuals like Hannah Witton, a YouTuber, broadcaster and writer who talks largely about sex, disability, sexual health and relationships, and Ruby Rare, a sex educator and writer who shares advice on Instagram. Such educators largely identify as queer, disabled and/or as women of colour, and they're amongst many leading the new wave of sexual education available to all young people with an internet connection, regardless of their location in this country and even this planet.

A more holistic sex education, both formal and informal, could indeed have helped me. If, when I was in Year 6, instead of only being taught about the technical reproductive process in a sex-segregated class (girls watched a video about periods and boys watched one about erections), we were also taught about consent, about how to speak out if something feels wrong, if someone has harmed you, perhaps I could have found the courage to speak to someone I trusted about the abuse I had experienced.

Alongside the stark introduction to patriarchal culture outlined earlier, these teen years were when repressed memories of my childhood abuse started finding their way to the front of my psyche. I wonder where I was, who I was with, when I first completely remembered. Perhaps there was never one first complete memory, perhaps it only ever came to me in the flashes and nightmares I know now; a jigsaw that finally became complete one day, though I can't remember when that day was.

Whenever I remembered the repressed memories, I swore to myself I would never tell anyone. I swore it would be my secret; my shame to carry with me for the rest of my life. This secret promise fell apart slowly over the next few years. Many survivors of childhood sexual abuse do indeed keep this promise to themselves, taking the shame into their late adulthoods or even their graves. The Office for National Statistics recently found that one in five survivors of rape or penetrative assault in childhood and one in four survivors of other kinds of sexual contact have never told anyone. Many survivors of sexual assault after the age of sixteen also tell no one, with nearly one-third of these victims not telling anyone about their experience. Society leads us to believe that being a survivor, especially of childhood abuse, is a shameful secret. Compounding the fact of childhood sexual abuse as shameful in itself is the fact that the majority of cases of childhood sexual abuse are committed by friends and family members of the children abused. How do you come to terms with your abuse when it was committed by someone you trusted? If you were led to believe that they weren't wrong, then it stands to reason that you must be.

I started by telling my friends. I'd approach it coyly, nervously. It would usually be when I was drunk or high, and I'd pose the question to my friends: 'Have you ever had anything really bad happen to you?' They would reply, drunken and confused, that they hadn't − had I? I would laugh it off, continue double-bouncing them

on the trampoline we were rolling around on at a Year
11 Leavers' house party. Rewind ten years; also, oddly,
on a trampoline. Are trampolines where I always almost
revealed my hidden traumas? At the age of eight or nine,
I sat with my childhood best friend, Richard. We were
having one of those deep conversations adults forget kids
have. We were talking about our biggest secrets. He
told me an innocent secret, and as a child whose biggest
problem was that his face was steeped with shame. He
asked me what my secret was – I told him it was too big
to tell him. He persisted, and I made something benign
up, something equally innocent to his. I wonder what
would have happened if I had told him about the abuse
then? Would he have tried to help me, would he have
told his parents, who then would have told mine?

At age seventeen, I began a relationship with the young
love of my life. We had been friends for years and had
finally confessed our feelings for one another. We meant
a lot to one another. It was with him that I finally began
speaking about my childhood abuse in full, could finally
speak some of the story without being blind-drunk or
high. It was as though being this close to a young male
figure, something I'd craved for so long, opened up some
form of trust within me – Freud would probably have
something to say about that. It must have been through
this gradual opening that I decided to tell my parents about
the abuse. Dramatically, I was at Glastonbury Festival
when I ultimately decided I was going to tell them. It
was a definite and certain decision. It was the Friday
morning and my best friend, Kirsty, and I were lazily
rolling around in our tent. She was on her phone; I was

listening to some music on my shitty brick-phone I used for festivals. I started crying, and Kirsty asked me what was wrong. I told her that I'd decided I was going to tell my parents. Kirsty, the first friend I'd first ever told about the abuse, was taken aback by this; she knew how seriously I had sworn myself to secrecy. The blue tent we were in became hotter and hotter as I explained to her why I wanted to do it. I had decided for numerous reasons, ones that I won't write about here.

In those few days between deciding to and telling my parents, a weight was assuredly lifted. I felt lighter and free, like life was finally going to get better. Days later, I did tell them. I won't rehash these wounds here, but all that needs to be known is that the telling helped heal some of those wounds and made others deeper. What's more important is that telling these other people in my life opened up the space within me to begin to heal. I began therapy half a year later, a journey I'm anticipating pursuing for the foreseeable future. I wrote about it and wrote about it and now here I am, seven years later, writing a whole book about it. I don't know who I'd be, where I'd be, if I was still harbouring those heavy secrets. Honestly, I don't know if I'd be alive. Even if telling people didn't immediately fix everything in my life, speaking the words I'd once deemed so impossible was a life-saving decision.

# 2

# Politics

# Chapter 4

# The Hashtag

Tarana Burke, youth worker, activist and tenacious survivor, founded the 'Me Too' movement in Alabama in 2006 to help survivors – mostly Black women and girls and other women of colour – heal from their abuse. The movement addressed the lack of resources for survivors of sexual violence by building a community of advocates, driven by survivors themselves, who came up with solutions to help deal with and prevent the violence. This original movement is still going strong, especially since its recent international galvanisation, and continues to expand global conversations and advocate for all survivors of sexual violence, hold perpetrators accountable and foster healing in communities.

This vital grassroots initiative spread globally in 2017, when #MeToo went viral across social media. Endless stories emerged of the abuse, harassment and harm that countless people had suffered at the hands of powerful people in multiple industries. The hashtag trended with millions of Twitter and Facebook posts. Various countries followed suit with their own hashtags – #YoTambien in Spain and Latin America, #BalanceTonPorc (expose your pig) in France. #MeToo started new conversations and reignited old ones. There were a few major stories that gained a lot of attention, like the sexual violence alleged against Harvey Weinstein, Donald Trump and Bill Cosby. Beyond these headline stories of celebrity, people all over the world, predominantly women, were saying 'me too'. They were saying that they had survived something that had been kept secret for so long. Perhaps it was a colleague on Facebook, a friend telling you over a coffee, or an idol of yours on Twitter; survivors were everywhere. Of course, we had always been everywhere, but we were finally speaking out and, more importantly, finally being heard. There was finally a space where we could exist in all our vulnerable and traumatised reality.

The #MeToo movement, along with the #TimesUp campaign in Hollywood, did so much to help the way we talk about and deal with sexual violence. Despite what the media showed, it wasn't just in elite sections of society either – in the USA, the Alianza Nacional de Campesinas (a women's farmworkers alliance) and other domestic workers highlighted the abuse rampant in their industries. McDonald's workers in the US went on strike against sexual harassment. These campaigns sparked long-overdue conversations, began to protect survivors from certain abusive people and saw formal justice for some (albeit extremely limited and nonetheless problematic). They made those who were outside of our personal 'whisper networks' aware that these things were happening all the time, everywhere. The movement also connected isolated survivors and provided a sense of widespread community. We could now truly begin to see that we weren't alone.

This movement for change wasn't just a standalone event back in 2017. There's a constant undertow of speaking out and holding people accountable; too many instances to denote in this chapter. It's ongoing and people are endlessly telling their stories and disclosing the pain they've lived with. In 2020, a sort of second 'Me Too' appeared to be occurring online. This outpouring seemed to erupt from a younger generation, from people who have come of age in the era of #MeToo. This was seen with the trend 'I was . . .', in which thousands of Twitter users started a thread on the ages at which they were sexually abused. Young women have also started speaking out on Twitter and Instagram about the harms they suffered at the hands of a younger generation of actors and musicians. Whilst the 2017 tsunami of #MeToo appeared to be holding mostly older generations accountable, younger men were now also being held to account. Men from indie bands, comedians and younger actors all felt the wrath of online accusations. Many of the women speaking out about their abuses were still teenagers during the first wave of #MeToo. They were the first to be socialised to know that we can speak up for ourselves, and that when we do, many people will listen.

This knowledge that we aren't alone, that there are so many others who've been through similarly terrible things, can at times become too much to deal with. It's a catch-22 – we don't want to be alone, and it comforts us to know that we aren't, but we don't want anyone else to feel this sort of pain or shame. Since time immemorial, the news cycle has contained awful stories, from war and famine to genocidal regimes and police brutality. This is all, obviously, quite distressing for our baby lizard brains to deal with on a frequent basis. But, in the past, we weren't so constantly connected, or expected to be so constantly connected to these news cycles. Now, we have regular alerts from news apps, we have Twitter trends and Instagram stories. We have every outlet covertly guilting us; if we aren't constantly up to date with the horrors of the world, then we are bad members of our community; we are negligent, we're complacent. We are made to be constantly aware of the hardness of the world around us; our pain and anger constantly being mirrored back to us on our iPhone screens. To see so many people share stories of the sexual violence they've survived can be triggering and overwhelming. Our minds simply aren't developed to consume this much information of trauma on a regular basis, especially if we ourselves have been through similar trauma. We may read a story strikingly similar to ours, and our bodies will go into overdrive, trying to protect ourselves from that familiar harm once more. Just the simple reminder that sexual violence is such a pervasive feature of our society can be too distressing. I have often found myself dissociating or temporarily breaking down after reading someone else's story. I see my pain reflected in theirs and it's too hard to look at directly; the fireball of trauma burning into our memories as the sun does to our corneas.

For all the good it did in spreading the message of survival, a key problem with the #MeToo movement was that it encouraged a society-wide focus on the monsters in the closet. As opposed to a nuanced focus on power structures – patriarchy, racism and capitalism, to name but a few – commentators often focused solely on the individual men at the centre of the most infamous allegations. These perpetrator-monsters at the centre were unpalatable; they were easy for the world to hate. They were just what we'd expected all along.

I want to make clear that these powerful men were violent and often devastatingly harmed their victims. That should, I hope, be clear from my writing. However, I want to ruminate on the fact that these men seemed to be so easy for us to hate. They fitted into racial, ableist and homophobic stereotypes we've all been taught. Harvey Weinstein and Bill Cosby became the ultimate monsters hiding in our closet. They could easily become the devil incarnate in the grim stories we heard; they were the monsters we'd always been told to be wary of. I wonder how the world would react if Prince Charming – a beautiful, pleasing, white man – was accused? I don't have to wonder for too long, as we've already seen it. Consider the numerous allegations against James Franco, Casey Affleck and countless other whispered-about men who are extremely beautiful and also allegedly extremely harmful in their abuses of power. They, to all intents and purposes, get away with it. The harm becomes easier to forget when it comes from a prettier hand. Rape culture has become defined by the elite society of disgusting and powerful men, as opposed to the pervasive power structure we all live in. As William Warwick for *The Gawker* says, 'If we are unable to stomach the fact that Woody is not a monster but a human being who did something monstrous, we will continue to stoke the fires of archetype, perpetuating the notion of the picture-perfect paedophile, the one whose evil shines through like a 100-watt black lightbulb.' We create these ultimate monsters of rape culture because to acknowledge that they are fellow humans among us is just too much for us to collectively bear. Instead, we pantomime them. The monsters are constantly behind those other victims we watch from the audience; we shout, 'He's behind you!', but can fail to see that the stage and set design themselves are the real horror.

The mainstream movement also often failed to make room for the nuances and complications that sexual violence holds. The hashtag and the media's coverage focused on the binaries – the perpetrator/victim; the accused/accuser; bad/good; men/women. This left little room for the way that abuse is often a cycle – people can both cause harm and be victims of harm themselves, as seen in the case of Asia Argento. Argento, an actor, was raped by Harvey Weinstein aged twenty-one, but she was also accused of rape by a man who had been a minor at the time of the alleged assault. People were confused. Were we still supposed to feel sorry for Argento? Was she cancelled too? The strict moral binary we'd been told to feel left us helpless in this scenario. Acknowledging that anyone can both be harmed and perpetrate harm themselves, oftentimes as a result of themselves being harmed, is an important step for society to take.

#MeToo often operated in naming and shaming harmful individuals. The reason for this was to hold perpetrators accountable and to inform and protect others from the risk of working with those harmful individuals. Its ultimate aim was often to disappear the accused altogether. But does this disappearing of people really work? It may assuredly protect people in their immediate sphere, for instance when a senior lecturer is fired from a university and their current students are protected. However, those harmful individuals have to go elsewhere, as Alison Phipps highlights in her book *Me, Not You*. The disappeared are swept to the side into other, perhaps less protected industries where other vulnerable workers may be exposed to their harm with less power to fight it. The people who have done harm aren't in fact disappeared, as many so desire. Further still, the culture that produced these monsters will continue. The phrase 'a few bad apples' often omits the latter half of the phrase, which is more appropriate here: 'A few bad apples spoil the bunch.' The bunch, rather, is what spoils the individuals – these harmful people are not anomalies. They were nurtured and socialised to harm people as they have done. The key problem is the culture; it's the power these individuals have had bestowed by society, and, as Jenny Holzer said, 'Abuse of power comes as no surprise.' Undoubtedly, individual agency has an important role to play – not every person in a position of power will rape and abuse. However, removing the bad few won't ultimately prevent the risk of more bad men from appearing in their places.

For all the stories we've heard, all the reports and commendations, we also hear the ensuing, vicious back-lash. We see the hot Twitter takes, people spitting out the label 'feminist' as synonymous with 'man hater'. The same people decry that the movement is a 'witch hunt' or 'lynch mob' – terms that are particularly ironic, seeing as witch hunts were historically misogynistic murders of non-conforming women and queer people, often those who spoke out against injustices, and lynch mobs were the racist public murders of Black men accused of committing crimes in the Antebellum South in the United States.

Depending on which circles we move in, we will see varying degrees of this backlash – I know I'm pretty lucky and cotton-wool-padded in my queer, leftist circles, both in my on- and offline life. I vividly remember first seeing both *The Atlantic* and the *New York Times*'s opinion pieces arguing that the accusation of sexual misconduct against comedian and actor Aziz Ansari was 'the worst thing to happen to the #MeToo movement' and why women (in this context, read: survivors) were 'dangerous'. In an article written for feminist online magazine *Bitch*, Ansari was accused of taking a woman on a date and pressuring her into sex in numerous ways, despite both verbal and non-verbal cues from the woman that she was not consenting to these sex acts. The responding opinion pieces argued that what had happened to Grace (not her real name) was a 'bad date' and that the allegations made against Ansari were part of a terrible feminist revolution that swept him up as an unlucky victim. They decried that his career was ruined – a bold claim dramatically disproven with his subsequent Netflix special, his international live show and an invite from Netflix to continue his dramedy series.

These critical opinion pieces broke me. Specifically, the one that aggressively victim-blames Grace for not being loud enough or strong enough to prevent what happened to her. That same piece sees this accusation as 'trivialising' the #MeToo movement. These discussions made me explode in anger and despair. It made me feel violent inside, made me spew certain misogynistic words at the article. Maybe this anger I had was so powerful because I saw myself in Grace's story, because I recognised the entitlement and complete disrespect of my personhood, recognised the way my body was seen solely as an object for my abusers' sexual pleasure. Maybe it's because I have been harmed in the past by an egotistical, faux-progressive man. It all felt too familiar. The reflection was too clear.

This isn't really about what Ansari did or didn't do, what his actions 'counted as'. Too much time has already been spent focused on the perpetrators and what they did or didn't do. This is about the way other people responded in disappointing ways to such accusations. It seemed from this story that the 'movement' itself had become divided about what was 'bad enough' for us to talk about. Even some of my favourite feminist thinkers contributed in damaging ways to this discussion, suggesting that what Ansari was accused of doing wasn't 'that bad' or 'bad enough' to be said in the same breath as other cases of sexual violence. The problem with that argument, along with shaming those who have experienced the forms of violence in question, is that it places instances of sexual violence within the hierarchy I talked about in the first chapter. It only allows sympathy, anger or action for the extreme – the rapes seen in the movies, only the most evil of evils. It suggests that being groped in your office is bad, but if we're touched non-consensually on a night out, then what else were we expecting? It tells us that being dragged down an alley and raped is clearly horrific but feeling forced to give oral sex to a man you went on a date with – a man you had the audacity to go home with – isn't really assault. It was just a 'bad date', so get over it. If someone says they feel like an experience of theirs was assault and that they feel violated, the response should be quite simple: believe them. Telling someone they weren't hurt won't make it so. It will only confuse and invalidate them, usually leaving them in further mental distress, deeper in the shame they've been told they should have. Another person saying that a painful experience didn't happen will never negate the fact that, for the survivor, it did.

What astounded me was that the *New York Times* journalist was so close to getting it. She begins her article with 'I'm apparently the victim of sexual assault. And if you're a sexually active woman in the 21st century, chances are that you are, too.' So. Close. People, of course, should be able to define what happened to them based on how they feel about it and how they experienced it. This journalist does not want to be forced to say she was assaulted in previous situations similar to the one Grace describes. That is completely fine, because that's what she wants. The point isn't to enforce victimhood on anyone, but to ensure that those who feel they have survived something harmful feel validated and capable of accessing support and community. To my unending amazement, this seems to have to be spelled out: if someone is in pain and feels harmed, please don't mock them. Whatever you want to call it – sexual assault, misconduct, harassment and so on – the fact is that many women and people of other marginalised genders, and indeed many men, are victims and survivors of some form of sexual violence. Sure, it might not be explicit, brutal rape. The key problem is that so many sexual encounters are harmful, painful and confusing. We weren't taught about concepts like enthusiastic and ongoing consent or non-verbal cues in sex education, so harmful things happen more frequently than many may assume. Almost all the women, non-binary people and many men I know who I have discussed this topic with have talked about at least one time they felt pressured and uncomfortable during sex. But, just as the backlash against Grace's story in *Bitch* showed, we're expected to get on with it, to get over it – because it happens to everyone, you're just being too sensitive!

As I discussed at the beginning of this book, I have had many euphemistic 'things' happen to me that I have had to shrug off for the sheer fact that I've just had even worse 'things' happen. Some of these 'things': I have woken up after being blackout drunk, next to the man I was dating who told me we had had sex, though I do not remember it; I have been drugged with an unknown substance in a club, and thankfully then saved by a friend before anything worse could happen; I have had male friends act sexually inappropriately towards me when they've been drunk. Even though I don't want to admit that any of these were 'serious' enough to call sexual violence, all of these instances were harmful and violent; they all contributed to the spectrum of sexual violence and rape culture that we live in.

Denouncers of #MeToo proclaim that there's an epidemic of false allegations across the Western world. Anxious men and defensive women retort that there are frequent cases of false allegations. Certainly, false allegations can occur. However, the Home Office estimates that only 4 per cent of cases of sexual violence in the UK are thought to be false. Studies elsewhere in the world estimate the rate between 2 and 6 per cent. So, in these rare cases, false allegations can indeed occur. A false allegation may indeed mean the accuser lied, but the statistics also include cases where explicitly conflicting evidence arises: for example, someone may go to the police if they're not sure an assault occurred whilst they were unconscious, but evidence of any assault comes back as negative in their rape kit. Using false allegations as a stance against the #MeToo movement is clearly an approach rooted in fear. Scared men and their allied women have become so terrified that they will be falsely accused, having been so misled by far-right media. They begin to realise the web of rape culture they're entangled in. Have they harmed someone before? Will they be held accountable? Instead of nurturing an atmosphere of accountability and healing in instances of harm, people who hold power are socialised to do whatever they can to protect their precious innocence. These men apparently become fearful of women, fearful of being alone with women in case they're accused of something. This stems from the fear of accountability and the brutal revelation that they must be aware of the space they take up in this world – the same way we've always had to be so aware.

Many critics of the #MeToo movement will also say that we can't take social media statements, trial-by-media or social opinion as absolute truth. They will say that due process is still needed to maintain hard-fought-for civil rights. Whilst protecting the accused, what these critics often skim over is the violence of the formal criminal justice system for the victim–survivor. What they skim over is the way in which powerful people usually silence less powerful people with money. The critiques of 'cancel culture' and trial-by-media are valid in many ways, such as the way shaming 'cancelled' people won't lead to any systematic change, but what the critics fail to supply us with is the current alternative reality of what justice we could try to seek instead.

The harbourers of rational discourse stress that trial by the media shouldn't be the norm, that denouncing 'due process' isn't the way forward. To some degree, I agree with this. I understand that trial by media oftentimes affects marginalised groups far more than it does more powerful groups. However, the problem is that alternatives aren't usually substantially given in these critiques. They solely denounce our current strives for social justice via these alternative methods. They fail to mention the real notions of transformative or restorative justice that we can turn to. It is all well and good to say people have a right to trial and presumed innocence, but where is the alternative structure to ensure that justice can still be sought for the survivors? When someone makes an allegation against someone who was sexually abusive, the accused may indeed be ostracised and experience social and material losses. But this is something that is also experienced by the accusers. These denouncers of #MeToo don't give enough space to the fact that a victim's testimony matters too. Critics on the left and right alike try to remind us of the need for corroborating evidence and due process - do they not realise how hard it is to find physical evidence in many instances of sexual assault? Notwithstanding the fact many acts of sexual violence leave no apparent physical marks of traumas, what about such atrocities as the 11,000 untested rape kits found in an abandoned warehouse in Detroit in 2009? After the backlog was finally cleared, 824 of the kits pointed to serial offenders. How many more rapes happened because of those forgotten kits? Victims themselves are often denied due process – put into a box of 'the lying woman' once again. Survivors are expected to expose their whole lives for the world to decide on their innocence. A survivor's testimony shouldn't have to be violated in similar ways to how their own bodies were violated for the sake of due process. We must seek alternative forms of justice, as opposed to the carceral, punitive justice we've been indoctrinated into believing as the only way.

Over the years, plenty of discussion has arisen over the possibility of separating the art from the artist. This isn't a new question – we've long asked if we can value and appreciate Pablo Picasso's artworks although he was a rampant misogynist, or whether we can appreciate Wagner's music even though he was an anti-Semite. Art is political; it matters what we consume, both philosophically, monetarily and, for survivors, emotionally. I myself can't consume media that features someone I know to be abusive. My favourite TV show used to be *Parks and*

*Recreation*, which sadly features a duo of #baddudes –
Louis C. K. and Aziz Ansari. My sophisticated technique
when they appear on screen is usually to fast forward
through their scenes. This is harder to do with Ansari
(part of the main cast) than C. K., but you'd be surprised
at how little is lost from the show's content without
Ansari's misogynistic character, Tom. I've never watched
a Polanski film and only watched half of *Annie Hall* when
I was a teenager (I stopped watching it because I thought
it was bad). I stop listening to certain musical artists when
I've heard credible things about their abuses of power.

I don't say all of this to exhibit my moral superiority,
but to show that, because of my trauma, I have to try to
avoid these works for the sake of my health. When I see
Ansari's face on a Netflix advert or a news story about
Woody Allen, I feel myself go into defence mode. I see
my assaulter's face, get transported back to the beach
from when I was eighteen. My trauma response is triggered, and I try hard to calm myself down. Why would I
purposely inflict these triggers on myself ? Separating the
art and the artist isn't just a matter of morality for many
people; the inability to separate the two is an undebatable
necessity for our self-preservation. This is not an ethical,
philosophical or even political decision – though it may
be those things too – but is simply an emotional response
to harmful situations that remind us of our own trauma.

As I've shown, I do understand the notion of being
intelligent, empathetic and understanding about all of
these things – paying attention to the binary of good and
bad people, or to the way rapists are turned into monsters
so we don't pay too close attention to the structures that

made them. I myself am anti-carceral (meaning I don't believe that incarceration and prisons are the solution to violence in the world; more on that later) and I do not believe anyone is intrinsically bad, but instead that we're all results of our socialisation, for better or for worse. That being said, there is still a special place I reserve for rage for those of us who've been so historically fucked over by abuses of power. This rage has a right to exist on its own as a pure and raw thing, before rationalism may kick in.

As I write this, comedian James Veitch has multiple allegations of sexual assault and rape against him, all of which he denies. His new HBO special has been dropped by the network. In a moment of schadenfreude, I feel manic glee bubble up from me as I read of his hardships. I admit to having a soft spot specifically reserved for the demise of shitty comedians, but a rushing rage will assuredly fill me every time I read of someone facing such allegations. The supposed witch hunt casts its influence over me, only this time, it's the witches doing the hunting. This doesn't necessarily make me a good person, but it does make me a person. Revenge isn't what I really want to choose, but it sometimes still rears its honest head out of my chest when my anger becomes me. When we're told we need to be civil and to calm down, when no form of justice is found, there is undoubtedly some joy in screaming vengeance from our rooftops and laptop screens.

#MeToo and the media fanfare around it can be contained within this 'outrage economy' that marks our modern times. I myself capitalised from this outrage

economy. Both creating my podcast with a major institution and writing this book have made me capable of
capitalising on my own trauma. I have undoubtedly
helped people with the work I've done, but nonetheless
participated in a problematic media world that has been
so damaging to so many victim–survivors. What does
it mean to capitalise off my trauma? To make my life's
work centre around the most difficult and traumatising
experiences of my life? At this present time in my life,
I can't imagine it any other way. I find fulfilment and
purpose in creating art around it, finding ways to share
my experience in the hope it can help to destigmatise the
subject for others. But part of me wonders how I will
feel in a few years. Will I become tired of being milked
for my trauma so many times? When I still get messages
from people opening their wounds to me, telling me
how much they need my help, will I still be able to do
it? Will I change my mind about showing my insides
to everyone, (over)sharing in the way I do? Will I read
back on this very paragraph and wonder how I could
have been so silly, my wariness staring me directly in the
face from these pages?

There is only so much you are allowed to show in
the public eye of being the go-to survivor. You can't
be too crazy, too much. You can't name your abuser,
can't identify them in any way. You can't proclaim
that all cops are bastards – that would be too political.
You can't talk about capitalism and neo-colonialism,
the way these things are interrelated with everything in
our modern life, for fear that you will be perceived as
being too scary and communist. Our pain and anger are

curated and represented with a neat bow on top. The institutions feel good about themselves – they've told our stories, with some parts redacted, they've made our voices heard. But what will these newly heard voices truly change? What have they changed so far? Perhaps it was all a red herring, the world returning to its comfortable place after the façade has fallen down. Or, perhaps it's slowly, gently shifting – tectonic plates of our rape culture peeling away from their core, moving us towards a future without this violence.

# Chapter 5

# Intersections of Violence

**Trigger Warnings: racism, misogynoir, slavery, transphobia, transmisogyny, ableism**

'Sexual violence doesn't exist in a vacuum – they are not just individual stories. They include our individual stories, but these stories are part of a larger web of violence in our societies: patriarchy, racism, colonialism and capitalism.'

Anuhya Bobba, *Wear Your Voice*

I'm a survivor of some really shitty things that have happened in my life. However, as a white, middle-class, cisgender-appearing person, the things I have survived have not been impeded by, or indeed been rooted in, my race, class or being transgender.

Women generally are at a higher risk of experiencing sexual violence, being five times more likely than men to be subjected to sexual assault. The crisis of sexual violence is one rooted in male supremacy and patriarchy. That being said, two other truths exist: any gender can be the victim of sexual violence, and some women are more at risk than others. One does not simply have the identity of 'woman' in isolation without other intersecting identities. For example, a woman may be Black, white, or otherwise racialised; gay, straight, bisexual or queer; cisgender or transgender; middle or working class; disabled or able-bodied. 'Womanhood' taken as a rigid, singular category fails to account for the many, very real variations that make up the vastly different lives of women. Our fight against sexual violence has to take into account more than gender disparity. Sexual violence exists within a complex social world of gender, race, class, ability and sexual relations. We can't talk about sexual violence without including the nuances and complications of our social world. Sexual violence is not a singular issue. As Audre Lorde puts it, 'There is no such thing as a single-issue struggle because we do not live single-issue lives.'

Sometimes it's hard to talk about the politics and identity aspects of sexual violence if we're not personally affected by them. When you feel traumatised every day, it can feel impossible to extend your view beyond yourself and your intense daily pain. But we need to extend our own outlook, for everyone's sake. This wider focus doesn't take away from our own personal trauma but allows for nuances and further complexities in how we can try to dismantle rape culture and its close allies: racism, transphobia, queerphobia and ableism (and a plethora of other violent power dynamics swirling around us). It's hard to think about. Survivors crave comfort and this side of it is uncomfortable. The most important thing in being an ally to other survivors is to listen to what they've been through. Listen to the different effects sexual violence has on different people and their communities, and advocate for them whenever you can. Let's follow the great Fannie Lou Hamer and her poignant statement: 'Nobody's free until everybody's free.'

In this chapter, I will cover some of the backgrounds and effects of sexual violence on different identity groups and communities. I've added subheadings so that survivors of the identity groups mentioned can skip parts should they want or need to – if you belong to those identity groups I mention that I don't belong to, you clearly know more about it than I do. It is by no means an exhaustive list, and I cover those I have most adequately researched (and with the latter two, experienced myself) – Black, trans, queer and disabled survivors and communities. There are a plethora of other identity groups and life experiences that affect the way we experience sexual violence. There is also so much more to say about the identity groups I cover, and I highly encourage you to read the books referenced, those books written by people of the backgrounds and communities I mention, and to do your own research to find out more on the nuances of different experiences.

The term 'intersectionality' was coined by Kimberlé Crenshaw in the late 1980s, but the concept has been used widely by Black feminist scholars for hundreds of years, all the way back to Sojourner Truth's speech 'Ain't I A Woman' in 1851. Intersectionality refers to the intersecting power dynamics present in social relations. It's a way of viewing power and privilege; seeing that no social identity is singular but instead 'intersects' in various ways with other identities one might have. Crenshaw visualises it effectively in her TED talk. In her example, a Black woman is being discriminated against by a hiring company, but the company defends their position, stating that they 'hire women' and 'hire Black people' – that is, Black men. Crenshaw makes the point that this Black woman lives at the intersection of two different identity positions and their resulting power inequalities in the social world. The Black woman isn't affected by just sexism or racism, but both – a sexist racism. We all have intersecting identities. None of us are singularly 'white', 'Black', 'straight', 'queer', 'woman' or 'man'. We are all affected by intersecting identities, and accordingly aided or abetted in the socially ordered world we live in. In terms of my own identity, I hold social power in being white in a white supremacist world, being middle class in a classist UK society and being cis-assumed in a cissexist world. I don't really identify as a cis woman, yet I still live with the privileges of being perceived as cis. I do not have social power in other ways: by being a woman in a patriarchal world, queer in a heteronormative world and disabled in an ableist world. However, because of my other privileged identity aspects, I do hold certain powers that fellow people in these social groups do not. As individuals with any identity that the world sees as 'lesser' or 'inferior', we must stay mindful and fight for those in our identity groups that are affected by other structural oppressions. Feminism, queer and gender-based violence activisms are redundant if they don't pay attention to and work to deconstruct the oppressive structures that harm women of colour survivors, Black survivors, queer and trans survivors, disabled survivors and working-class survivors.

## Race and Sexual Violence

Women of colour are statistically more at risk of experiencing sexual violence, being affected in various ways across ethnic lines; 84 per cent of indigenous women in the Americas are survivors of violence and over half of them have experienced intimate partner violence; 77 per cent of Latina women say that sexual harassment in the workplace is a major concern. Women from all over the Asian continent experience fetishisation and hyper-sexualisation in a Western context, rooted in colonial and military histories. The history of white supremacy and colonialism mean that racialised women have suffered sexual violence in different ways from white women. Whilst different ethnic groups and cultures have their own nuanced experiences, I will here focus on the way Black women have been affected by sexual violence. For a much deeper and more nuanced exploration of the way women of colour have been affected by white supremacy and violence, please see Ruby Hamad's book *White Tears/Brown Scars: How White Feminism Betrays Women of Colour.*

In 1962, Malcolm X proclaimed that 'the most disrespected person in America is the Black woman. The most unprotected person in America is the Black woman. The most neglected person in America is the Black woman.' Over fifty years later, this still rings true, not just for America, but for the Western world generally. Today, Black women and girls are still disproportionally more likely to be harmed. Women like those whose stories we hear in the documentary, *Survivng R. Kelly*. Women like Oluwatoyin Salau, a nineteen-year-old activist who was raped and murdered in July 2020. There are numerous reasons for the disproportionate victimisation of Black women. Firstly, as referred to in Crenshaw's example above, Black women and other women of colour simultaneously experience sexism and racism.

The term 'misogynoir' was coined in 2008 by Moya Bailey and Trudy (aka @thetrudz) to describe the anti-Black, racist misogyny experienced by Black women. This includes the sexual violence committed against Black women. The quote placed at the beginning of this chapter encapsulates the intricate, nuanced histories that have brought us to this world entrenched with misogynoir. These histories include the transatlantic slave trade, during which an estimated 12.5 million people were kidnapped by colonists from their homelands on the African continent, auctioned off by slavers and forced to work in fatal conditions on American lands. For Black women, part of this horrific history included their rape at the hands of the masters who enslaved them. Black people were seen as property, Black women were seen as sexual property and the children born of them were also seen as white slavers' property. The narrative constructed to justify these unfathomable atrocities was that the enslaved peoples were inferior and inhuman.

We live with by-products of these constructions to this day. After the slave trade was officially abolished (although it was seen to continue up until the 1960s), Western society was, and is, still deeply racist. Lynching of Black men accused (often falsely, although that shouldn't matter) of crimes, including rape, against white people were common in the early twentieth century. Throughout the twentieth century, southern states of the USA enforced segregation between Black and white communities, and the supposed notion of 'separate but equal' was assuredly false: Black people were still seen by white society as inferior. To this day, racism, anti-Black violence and misogynoir are entrenched throughout Western globalised societies. As countless activists across the past century have shown, racism and white supremacy exists all around us in insidious ways as well as in brutal, obvious ways, such as in cases of police brutality, the Windrush Scandal, the Grenfell Tower fire, the aftermath of Hurricane Katrina, the Syrian refugee crisis and hostile immigration policies. These scandals and crises are seemingly endless, as the capitalist white supremacist machine of society keeps churning. Recent movements such as Black Lives Matter, started in 2015 and co-founded by survivor Alicia Garza, demand that the white world wakes up to the injustice suffered daily by Black people and other people of colour.

As discussed earlier in this book, the #MeToo movement is owed to a Black woman: Tarana Burke. Burke created the movement not as a mass reckoning for people in powerful industries. She originally created it as she realised the power held within those two simple words between survivors: 'Me Too'. She'd heard those words and had said them herself frequently amongst young Black women who experienced a nuanced shame about the violence they'd survived – both from wider white society and from their closer Black communities. We owe #MeToo to a Black woman, yet the movement only took off at the level we see today when white actor Alyssa Milano tweeted the phrase. It cannot be denied that the global movement created impressive change and started conversations on both large and small scales, yet the world media focused most of its attention on the white celebrity women of #MeToo. This reinforced the myth of the perfect victim and what she looks like. This perfect victim is coded as white, cis, wealthy and determinably innocent.

As referenced in Crenshaw's 1991 article, Professor Valerie Smith theorised a hierarchy that 'holds certain female bodies in higher regard than others', for instance, white feminine bodies over their Black counterparts. In anti-rape activism, the racial dimensions of many instances of sexual violence are left out, unless it's the perpetrator who isn't white – and in those cases it's paid attention to disproportionately. Tarana Burke realised quickly that she had to insert herself rightfully as the founding leader of the movement. If she didn't, she risked having her life-long project (that was due to be launched a few months after Milano's igniting tweet) overshadowed by the white, mainstream co-optation of that very work. Burke's work is still thriving, as she ensures the key mission of the movement is still achieved – connecting survivors with the resources they need for healing and preventing future harms. As well as still acting as executive director of the official 'Me Too' movement, she also acts as the senior director for Girls for Gender Equity in New York.

★

What writers like Crenshaw, with campaigns like #SayHerName, and activists like Burke want to remind people of is the forgotten Black women who suffer at the hands of racism and sexism concurrently. As Tarana Burke states in *Surviving R. Kelly*, 'Black girls don't matter [enough].' Mikki Kendall then argues '[We] don't perceive young black women as innocent, as deserving of protection. Somehow, it's their fault.' Black women have historically been constructed as 'Jezebels' in the white world – always up for sex, promiscuous and emotionally strong. Just as Black men were constructed in the social story as violent, Black women were similarly constructed as hypersexualised. This plays into societies' Madonna/whore or good/bad woman dichotomy. With Black women stereotyped as hypersexualised, Crenshaw explains that they're 'pre-packaged as bad women' and, correspondingly, bad women can't be raped. This still has impacts – a 2017 report from Georgetown University found that Black girls are less likely to be believed than their white peers when they report rape because they appear 'less innocent'.

What Burke's original 'Me Too' movement showed was that Black women need specific support mechanisms in place to help them heal from sexual violence. With anti-rape activism often being white-dominated, specific spaces need to be given to survivors depending on their complex lived experiences – spaces like Imkaan in the UK, an organisation dedicated to addressing violence against Black and minoritised women and girls; and spaces like Sistah Space, a specialist domestic violence service run by and dedicated to survivors of African heritage. Further, our contemporary fight against racism and our pursuit to be anti-racist must include dismantling misogynoir-laden stereotypes and tropes. As the Combahee River Collective stated in 1977, 'If Black women were free, it would mean that everyone else would have to be free since our freedom would necessitate the destruction of all the systems of oppression.'

## Gender, Sexuality and Sexual Violence

### Trans Survivors

Trans people – both women, men and those who don't ascribe to binaries – are more at risk of experiencing sexual violence. Accurate data on trans people's experiences with sexual violence are scarce and unreliable – much more is needed to substantially try to help these communities. What we do know is that the 2015 US Transgender Survey found that 47 per cent of transgender people are sexually assaulted at some point in their lives. These rates rise with trans people of colour. If a trans person had been a sex worker, been homeless and/or they were disabled, rates of sexual violence were still higher. What we also know is that the individual experiences trans people try to tell us about – the way they're assaulted and abused in broad daylight; the way they're attacked by their sexual partners for 'hiding' their physicality. Despite these horrific figures, trans people suffer a dearth of resources. At the time of writing, there is only one anti-sexual violence charity in the UK – Galop – which is specifically dedicated to the needs of trans survivors.

Despite this lack of resources, and a lack of resources for survivors generally, the past decade has seen a galvanising of anti-trans activists attempting to further exclude trans people, especially trans women, from accessing support services. Although on the ground in crisis centres trans women are often helped when there is enough space for them, transphobic media campaigns have attempted to turn the public against trans women. A recent proposal to scrap reforms to the *Gender Recognition Act* would include limiting trans people's access to single-sex services unless they've had surgery, which is both a transphobic and classist requirement.

Let's take a moment to debunk some of the common transphobic narratives seen in British politics and the media. Trans exclusory separatists (TES, also known as TERFs*) root sexual violence primarily in biology, rather than the intersecting power relations that mark our social lives. On these grounds, they argue for cis women-only spaces and to prevent people from self-identifying as their gender. As Julia Serano writes in *Whipping Girl*, the biological justification of excluding trans women from women's spaces is inherently transphobic and transmisogynist† as it exhibits prejudiced aversions to trans women's anatomies/penises, conflates being transgender with sexual deviancy and excludes unconventional women's bodies from spaces that are both safer for them and affirming of

---

* I use this label as opposed to TERF in line with Viv Smythe who coined both terms.

† An intersection of transphobia and misogyny that targets trans women.

their identities. As told in the anthology *Written on the Body,* 'transmisogyny means that trans girls are identified with violence'. A slogan of TES is 'no unexpected penises', which 'evokes an organ with a life of its own, which is threatening because it is hidden (maybe, like the stranger rapist, it might jump out from the darkness)', Alison Phipps writes. It is possible that a small minority of predatory men will walk into women's changing rooms to harm women, but these cis men aren't trans women, and stopping people from self-identifying as their gender wouldn't stop such situations from occurring anyway.

As *gal-dem* reports, a 2018 *Guardian* investigation found that Ireland, which introduced self-determination in 2015, has seen 'no evidence' of new legislation leading to men 'falsely declaring themselves female'. Further, the exclusion of trans women with penises from single-sex spaces contains within it the assumption of normative heterosexuality, as the exclusion is justified on the grounds of keeping single-sex spaces non-sexual, implying that people with penises (i.e. 'men' in this context) harbour the natural inclination to sexually dominate their female counterparts in a heterosexual world. This exhibits both heteronormativity, by assuming people with penises would always be sexually attracted to women, as well as the patronising stereotype that women as a class are weaker, so thus must be protected from the physically stronger male.

Any gender can rape or abuse, and any gender can be victimised by violence. Violence belongs to no gender, although women (both trans and cis) are more likely to be subjected to violence. Sexual violence is about power and control, usually stemming from cisgender male dominance over feminised bodies – it's not about gender variations and gender non-conforming individuals. Writer Xoai Pham responds to transphobic media narratives that '[undermining] trans women's well-being does not make cis women more safe; it just makes all women more fearful. If our ultimate goal is to protect women, we should be fostering solidarity among us, so we protect one another, rather than emphasizing unfounded ideas.' Rather than pitting cis and trans women against each other, we should all work towards trying to make the world a safer place for one another.

Even when trans women can attend women's crisis centres, it can still be difficult for them to access substantive help, as rape counsellors may not have much training in dealing with the nuances that come with trans people's experience with sexual and domestic violence. Even if the binary spaces are there to help survivors, trans people are often left in a bind. For example, trans men may have to invalidate their identities to get a safer form of help by attending women's rape crisis centres and shelters. As *gal-dem* reports in their whistleblowing piece on transphobia in the violence against women and girls (VAWG) sector, two things are needed for progress: specialised training in trans inclusion for those working on the frontline supporting women, and a way for organisations to reassure trans survivors that they're trans inclusive. This has already started happening in Scotland, with training sessions and exclusive digital badges for organisations' websites to try to show they're a safe space for all survivors. To include trans people within already-existing binary services is also just the beginning; the next step is to ensure tailored services, with specially trained counsellors and carers. Trans women, men and anyone identifying on the non-binary spectrum deserve specialised and attentive care to heal from sexual violence, in the same way cis women are given the chance to.

## Queer Survivors

Being queer is assuredly a risk factor for sexual violence: over half of bisexual people have experienced sexual violence and double the number of gay men are sexually assaulted in comparison to their straight counterparts. In my personal life, a large majority of the survivors I know are queer. There's a definite link between being subjected to violence and being queer. In many cases, this link is a direct one – people are sexually violated because of violent prejudice against their sexuality. Corrective rape is the term used for cases where a queer person is raped by the opposite sex to 'correct' them into heterosexuality. Further, queer people are often fetishised and perceived as hypersexualised under the gaze of heterosexual people. Homophobic hate crimes against queer women can occur when they refuse to perform for the straight male gaze, as happened on a London bus in 2019 to a queer femme couple, and as happened to me and a woman the same year. Whilst I have only ever had positive intimacies with other women and gender-non-conforming people, it also needs to be said that sexual assault and rape within the LGBTQ+ community happens. The stigma around rape and survival is already profound, so when it's committed by someone else in the queer community, the stigma is compounded by queerphobia and various myths like 'women can't rape women'. If you add the stigma of rape to the stigma of being queer, the reality becomes a cruel and silencing world that invalidates you from every angle.

I also think there's another, more indirect link between survival and queerness. Many of the people I know who are both queer and survivors, including myself, realised their queerness after the fact of sexual violence. I had always known I was queer, but only came out to other people after the most recent assault. A man I know had only been with women until he 'came out' about his sexual abuse and soon after 'came out' in his queerness. Cruel cynics and homophobes alike could taunt that the experiences of sexual violence 'made us' queer. But I think there's a positive, deeper link: the 'coming out'. Through the internal struggles of societally imposed shame of sexuality alongside the shame instilled in being a survivor, the strength of coming out as either one can open up space for the other. Once I'd started being open about my survival and the things I'd endured, from sexual abuse to mental illness, I realised there was nothing holding me back from being open and proud about my queer identity.

As a survivor throughout my life, I had been led to turn inwards, to question myself, for better or for worse, about who I was and how my experiences had shaped me. I was made to see the tears in society's false reality; the way violence can be surprisingly close to the surface, the way someone you love can hurt you so fundamentally, the way your femininity and vulnerability can be used as a weapon against you. These realisations helped reveal the plasticity of the world, the way not everything has to be as it seems. The way all life is queer, in both the original and contemporary sense of the word. The life-shattering, life-building fact of child sexual abuse and rape in adulthood changed the fabric of my perspective to make me realise I had always been queer.

## Disabled survivors

In fights for social justice and resistance, conversations often fall short in knowing how to talk about disabled people and their experience of the world. We forget that sexual violence isn't just psychologically, invisibly, silently affecting. We tend to miss out the fact that disabled people – no matter their gender, but especially disabled women – are more at risk of sexual violence, and people can indeed be disabled, in various different ways, by sexual violence. Disabled women are three times more likely to be assaulted than able-bodied women. People who are inclined to abuse their power over others are more likely to do so if the person is disabled, because it can both be easier for them to commit the harm in the moment and because they may also believe they can get away with it in the aftermath. In conversations around street harassment and sexual harassment in public spaces, the people often forgotten about are those who are physically disabled. Disabled people are generally seen by able-bodied society as objects of pity. Whether it's being touched non-consensually, being asked intrusive questions or being unable to quickly get away from dangerous situations, physically disabled people are affected in complicated ways that able-bodied people don't usually have to think about.

Further, sexual violence can also occur in medical contexts. Similarly to how sexual violence can occur at the hands of police officials, medical officials can subject those under their power to degrading sexual invasions. Abusive medical practitioners can sexually abuse their patients, but other common practices can also be seen to be sexually violent when looked at in their brutal realities. Leah Lakshmi Piepzna-Samarasinha exemplifies this reality in *Beyond Survival*, offering up the overlooked violence of 'medical stripping in hospitals, to medical experimentation, to the genital mutilation of intersex people; from forced treatment, restraints, and chemical or psychiatric surgery, to forced sterilization, or to simply never being asked before being touched by a medical provider'.

When we talk about sexual violence, we also don't tend to talk of the numerous ways we can be disabled and chronically ill in the aftermath. I live with complex PTSD and chronic health conditions linked with the trauma I've survived. As mentioned previously, I have in part been disabled by my previous sexual trauma, but I've also had these disabilities, painfully and unjustly, used against me. This has happened twice, in two different yet connected contexts. During one of my assaults, I had a panic attack during the consensual sex preceding the assault. The man feigned support and care. Seconds later, he sexually assaulted me. He decided to use my vulnerability to assert his power in achieving his pleasure. I continued to have a severe panic attack, unable to move, throughout the various parts of the assault. As he was assaulting me, perhaps in one of the intermittent breaks (my memory is very hazy now; my brain protects me), he told me to 'get over myself'; he told me that I was 'crazy'.

Almost a year later, after I reported this assault to the police and the investigation was taking place, I was talking to my police officer about this fact. I had just recounted my witness statement, when afterwards I asked her off-the-record if the fact that I'd had a panic attack during the assault would affect the investigation and potential trial. I asked this in relation to how it could help my case – how it could perhaps represent the way the accused had taken advantage of a person in mental distress, had violated a vulnerable person, further showing the damage he had caused to me on that insidious night. She interpreted my question in another, much more sinister, way. She responded, 'Yes, it could potentially be used against you, as it could weaken your credibility. They could argue that you weren't of sound mind to know what was really happening.' Once again, I was made to understand, point blank, just how much the system is against us. The system mirrored exactly what my abuser had led me to believe: that my mental illness was making me unbelievable, that I wouldn't be believed precisely *because* I am mentally ill. If the system uses survivors' disabilities against them, how is there supposed to be any justice?

All of the identity groups mentioned in this chapter are affected in different ways by rape culture and the inter-secting power dynamics present in society. However, there are some commonalities between all of them. The most glaring commonality to me is the entitlement the world feels towards 'othered' bodies. Whether that's Black women's bodies, trans bodies, disabled bodies or queer bodies, society has taught people that such different bodies are public property. Any body that doesn't fit the perceived standard norm can be seen as 'fair game' for public, cis male attention. They can be touched on public transport, asked intrusive questions, harmed in various ways because they don't matter to the world as much as their normative counterparts. These bodies aren't seen as having boundaries and are devalued in our society, so they're seen as more acceptable to violate.

A further commonality between all the above groups is the lack of funding present for the specialist services so urgently needed by them. The domestic and sexual abuse sector is already on its knees with funding cuts – one in four refuges in the UK have lost all government funding in the last decade of austerity and 86 per cent of the reduction in government spending was in spending on women. When survivors generally are having their resources depleted, how can we ensure that survivors from certain backgrounds receive the vital specialist care they so deserve? We need to ensure care and healing for all in the ways they need and want in the aftermath of sexual violence. This shouldn't be a utopian dream but should be a reality we can strive towards. It's on the horizon, and all we have to do is begin to walk towards it.

# 3

# Minds and Bodies

# Chapter 6

# A Complex Condition

In the shadow years, between the ages of six and fourteen, the memories of the abuse would come to me as an imprint. A fossil in my mind of the bad things I had been made to do. I remember they would come to me suddenly; a flash. Then, just as abruptly, I could grasp them, contain them. I'd shove them at the back of my mind's closet, hoping they wouldn't spill out again too soon. I still have this skill, where I can think about it and not think about it at the same time. I can see it in my mind's eye, hold it, and dissociate at the same time. I've always seen it that my brain formed different pathways from 'normal' brains. I envision my six-year-old brain forming labyrinths as a way to cope, hiding from my abuse, misfiring neurons to protect me. Though I'm unsure of the exact neuroscience behind the mechanisms of my neural pathways, my conception of my brain developing special coping mechanisms has been confirmed by a diagnosis of complex PTSD. Originally diagnosed with PTSD a few years ago when I attended The Havens, the 'complex' part was a revision made by psychologists who understood the extent of the various interrelating abuses I've survived from childhood into adulthood. It was originally speculated that I may have bipolar type II – a form of bipolar characterised by drastically fluctuating moods, without mania – but the diagnosis of a mood disorder was slowly seen to be intimately linked with my historic trauma.

Post-Traumatic Stress Disorder (PTSD) is an anxiety 'disorder' that develops after experiencing or witnessing a traumatic event, though I think it's worth questioning why we denote a reasonable response to life-threatening scenarios a 'disorder'. This trauma could be rape or sexual assault, a car crash, military combat, or a traumatic childbirth. When we go through these situations, hormones such as cortisol and adrenaline are released to help us survive, or to help us experience the least amount of pain. Our body–mind – a term popularised by disabled theorists, such as Eli Clare, to emphasise the interdependence and inseparability of the body and the mind, as opposed to the separate notions of mind and body in popular Western thought – can respond to this initial threat in a number of different ways, including fight, flight, freeze, flop and/or appease. The first four are quite self-explanatory, but the last, also known as 'friend', is when an individual may try to appease the attacker (if there is one in the given situation) to try to prevent even more harm occurring. For instance, someone being sexually assaulted may ask the attacker to use a condom to prevent further future harms of pregnancy or infections. These responses happen at any age – they're our bodies' physiological reaction. This may seem obvious to some, but I only recently realised the way I was covertly victim-blaming of my six-year-old self. Despite my robust knowledge of trauma, I didn't fully comprehend that my six-year-old self too would have responded by freezing and dissociating as a form of self-preservation. I forgot that these responses aren't socialised, but physiological. The fact that my six-year-old self reacted by freezing and dissociating shows that you can't predict how you'll react – it's solely up to your body.

PTSD develops when our bodies continue releasing these stress hormones, believing that they're still protecting us from imminent harm. Although we may be out of harm's way – PTSD may continue or even develop years after an incident – our bodies remain hypervigilant and easily startled, attempting to keep us safe. Although it comes with incredibly difficult realities, sometimes I find solace in knowing that my condition stems from my body-mind trying to keep me safe. PTSD changes the way we deal with emotion, memory and reasoning, and their corresponding areas of the brain. Alongside hypervigilance (the state of always being 'on edge') come aspects like flashbacks, nightmares, trust problems, anger, depression and suicidal feelings.

Flashbacks can be visual, physical, emotional or sensual; for example, I have flashbacks to the way the room smelled where I was abused as a child. These varying flashbacks show how trauma can 'scramble' these memories. During flashbacks, it's believed that our frontal lobe shuts down, meaning we lose our ability to express these feelings or images and our sense of time and location (van der Kolk, 2015). The emotional brain takes over and we go into overdrive, reacting in various ways in our actual realities.

When I have panic attacks, I can't explain what's going on inside my head. I can hardly talk, I cry and my limbs shake. This is because the emotional brain takes over and our other 'rational' brain (which can usually match up with the emotional brain in our non-panicking moments) loses control. This mechanism often also happens in the traumatic situation itself, our emotional 'lizard' brain taking over to try and protect us. This means that the memory itself is processed in a different way from normal memories, and we remember odd bits and pieces: the smell, the lighting, a certain phrase. As van der Kolk writes in *The Body Keeps the Score*, 'Traumatic memories are fundamentally different from the stories we tell about the past. They are dissociated: the different sensations that entered the brain at the time of the trauma are not properly assembled into a story, a piece of autobiography.'

Although I had experienced the symptoms of PTSD to varying degrees throughout my life, I still felt like the diagnosis wasn't fully capturing my experience. I'd lived with all of the things above, but I also had extreme emotional instability. As I mentioned, it had been considered whether I had a form of bipolar for the extreme highs and lows I would feel week to week, day to day, perhaps even hour to hour. I also had intense relationship problems, becoming anxiously attached to any romantic partner and often falling into a pit of deep depression at any sign of rejection, whether from partners, friends or jobs. I'd also experience intense dissociation; not being able to control myself when things became 'too much', I'd lie on my floor crying, unable to move for hours when I was in the depths of depression. Although this last aspect is similar to what I've described above in a classic PTSD flashback, these instances often felt significantly rooted in the emotional response as opposed to solely being a traumatic memory response.

It was upon researching an essay for my master's degree that I discovered 'complex PTSD' (or c-PTSD) and subsequently suspected I had it. C-PTSD develops when someone has survived early developmental, severe, repeated and/or ongoing abuse. A month or so later, I was formally diagnosed with it by secondary-care psychologists. These psychologists explained c-PTSD in a somewhat simple way to me that has stuck. Consider a Venn diagram of PTSD (as described above) and another condition called Emotionally Unstable Personality Disorder (EUPD), also known as borderline personality disorder (which can be argued as being a loaded and sexist diagnosis in itself, but I digress). Traits of c-PTSD essentially exist at the intersection of these conditions, sitting somewhere in between the two. There is no direct science to it; some people may have traits more characteristic of EUPD, some of PTSD, and individuals may fit more in line with either one condition at different points in their lives, but c-PTSD is its own distinct condition from both of the others. The condition is, as its name might suggest, complex. That's the exact point of the definition: what we experience is a complex set of post-traumatic stress symptoms. Alongside the PTSD symptoms, survivors of c-PTSD experience emotional instability, a higher risk of suicidality, feelings of isolation and mistrust, and a tendency for emotional flashbacks. Emotional flashbacks are where you intensely re-experience emotions that formed strongly when you experienced the trauma: it could be feelings of anger, fear, shame. We often aren't aware when we're experiencing emotional flashbacks as they can appear when we are triggered by an already difficult experience in life; for example, a relationship break-up or an argument with a friend. My floor-crying episodes usually overcome me when something difficult has happened, and my body-mind falls back into the familiar pattern of complete emotional breakdown.

C-PTSD doesn't really 'make sense'. One week I will be fine, functional, capable of writing a whole essay or chapter; the next I will want to die. One evening I will be crying, unable to breathe; the next morning I will laugh and make jokes at work. One week I will spiral into doom, drink a bottle of wine and do lines of cocaine; the next week I will stay in bed watching shark documentaries and fall asleep at 9 p.m. Some weeks the memories are too loud, too bright; other times, I forget they happened at all (though my body always remembers). Some days I want to live for ever and love the world so much it hurts my cheeks to smile so much; other days I can't stop thinking about slitting my wrists open or walking into oncoming traffic. Triggers make things worse – a joke about abuse here, a familiar face there, but often there is no such immediately identifiable trigger apparent.

In the midst of writing this chapter, I have a 'triggered' episode — I'm always uneasy about how to phrase it. Is it too long to say the full truth, that I was reminded of my rape three years ago? That my whole being was dragged back into the fear of that night and the year of institutional trauma that occurred in the aftermath, the underlying legal trauma I live with to this very day? What actually happens is a roundabout way of being triggered – I interact with someone on the internet who I then realise is connected to the man who assaulted me. That's how these triggers often work; the smallest connection, the slightest recognition that you and your abuser are still living in the same city, the same world, can set you off. I want to tell this person the truth about this man they know. I plan it out and call on friends for their opinions. I ultimately decide against telling this person because of the potential legal repercussions I cannot risk occurring for my own safety. The anger and fear subsume me; it is not just the fear of how he harmed me that night, but the fear that he could dismantle my life further, quite literally as an agent of the patriarchy, that he could in all actuality try to place a legal 'gag order' on me (that phrase seems aptly violent in these cases) that could potentially prevent me from writing this very book. In this particular episode, I became scared of going outside for fear of the men I might see. My trauma response is definitively sexist: if I see a man, my body freezes up and I often turn and walk the other way. If it's a woman or a child, or even if a man is with either of these two 'safe' strangers, my body relaxes, shoulders dropping and jaw unclenching, I'm even happy in my perceived safety. I rationally know that not all men will hurt me. However, I don't think my wariness of male strangers is an irrational response to surviving previous violence, or even just to being a feminised body in a misogynistic world. I will not try to therapise this out of myself; my wariness acts as my protection – it's not 'just my trauma talking'. My trauma may indeed have created an overdrive of hypervigilance in my responses, but it does so with good reason. In our current world, I know my body-mind will never be completely safe. I will always have to be on edge, as will all my fellow femmes, as violence could always be just around the corner. This is not catastrophising; this is our reality.

These episodes also bring with them the self-hatred and a subsequent reviling of the people who love me that I have come to know so well. I will turn inwards in an effort towards self-preservation. I might ask a friend for help and if they cannot do it that day, it encourages me to make a promise to myself that only I can help myself, that no one cares about me, that all my friends are evil and that I deserve to be alone in life. When I emerge from my episodes, I see this as the saddest aspect. My friends are my chosen family, and I love them so, so dearly. Sometimes I have to fight hard to hold myself back from releasing my trauma onto them. I envision leaving the group chats, telling them I never want to speak to them again, throwing my phone onto concrete so they can't contact me, and more importantly for me in those moments, so they all worry about me. It is selfish and it is manipulative. Even if I don't really follow through with those actions, the thoughts course through me. This is the ugly side of being traumatised, the side we don't like to discuss. We try to protect ourselves in ways that are terrifying, and often, if one can't restrain oneself in the bitter throes of it, in ways that can be life-destroying. We are not always precious, soft and quiet – we can be angry, poisonous, screaming at the people who love us to fuck off. Van der Kolk writes: 'trauma can turn the whole world into a gathering of aliens', and one of the most terrifying aspects is when even the people you love, the people who've helped you survive, become those aliens to you too.

Nightmares are one of the common symptoms of PTSD. As someone with c-PTSD, accordingly, my nightmares have also become quite complex, both in content and effect. My bad dreams are frequent, occurring a few nights a week. As a teenager, before I had any treatment for my mental illnesses, I would have frequent night terrors – usually where a creature or person would be above me in my bed. I would jump out of bed (in waking life) and flee out of my room, coming to consciousness to realise it had only been a terror. I still get these now, although less often. The most recent one comprised some sort of circular bug – it somehow reminded me of images that trigger trypophobia, the fear of irregular holes or bumps in organisms. This bug or being was crawling up my hand, onto my arm, cocooning me. Everything in these dreams looks exactly the same as my reality; it is my room, my bed, my body. I jump up and out of my bed in terror. Just as quickly, I realise it's a dream. I go back to bed and fall asleep. These nightmares are plainly terrifying, yet another type of nightmare – the mundane nightmare – comes to me more often. I frequently have dreams of being assaulted or being trapped with my abuser, though fear isn't specifically felt as a result – the scenario just plays out as normal. The man who most recently assaulted me lingers as a spectre within these dreams; the benign antagonist. His face looms on the TV or he is introduced to me as a mutual acquaintance. In one dream we are walking down a tree-lined street and he tries to touch me – I tell him no; I tell him to get away from me. He almost listens. In another of these dreams, getting scarier now, we have to live together, share a bed. He won't leave. In another, he creeps around a bookshop I'm in, his face morphing multiple times; it is him around one corner, a doppelgänger around another. The most recent one told the story of him taking me to court and suing me for talking about my assault. I have to see his face and the face of his imagined lawyers.

How do you deal with these bad dreams that play out as a bad episode of a TV show? There is no looming monster, no ghosts or murderers. There is indeed a rapist, but the rapist is so normal that he has seeped into your psyche. How do you cope when you get stuck in lengthy dreams of living with your abuser in a one-bedroom flat? Since childhood, I have been able to awaken myself from truly terrifying nightmares. It's a nifty trick I learned after a recurring nightmare I'd have of Ursula from *The Little Mermaid* kidnapping me into a sea cave. I hear myself calling my own name from the depths of sleep and I can force my eyes open to reality. However, with these more mundane nightmares, my body doesn't register that I am in a nightmare. My mind doesn't come to rescue me from my own subconscious. These mundane nightmares don't need analysing; they are plain and clear in their messages. They tell me that I will never get substantive justice. They tell me that there are people who think I am lying and who will gaslight me endlessly. They tell me that there is a possibility the terrible could happen again.

They tell me that even I don't believe myself sometimes. They tell me his spectre still remains, deep within me.

Although distressing, my body recognises such dream-scapes as 'normal' because they *are* normal in our world. Undoubtedly they are horrible and torturous, but only as torturous as the c-PTSD that I live with in my waking life. I've started telling my partner about these dreams when I feel the urge to, otherwise I repress the dream as soon as I wake up, scared of focusing on it or remembering it too well. I tell myself that if I don't think of it, I will forget, as one does with most normal dreams. But these dreams shouldn't be normal. They are ugly and violent; they feel normal only in this nightmarish lived reality of being a survivor in rape culture.

C-PTSD is a relatively new diagnosis. Discussions of the condition have been in circulation within psychology since the 1990s, with many psychologists backing up research that defines c-PTSD as its own distinct condition from PTSD, with its own symptoms, causes and treatment options. However, mainstream medicine and society often still struggle to recognise it as a condition. The World Health Organisation only introduced it to the ICD-11 (the international classification of diseases) in 2019. The DSM5, another leading diagnostic manual especially dominant in the USA, still doesn't recognise it as its own distinct condition. This causes major problems for survivors with c-PTSD in countries like the USA where the accuracy of a diagnosis is vital for healthcare insurance. The recentness of c-PTSD being recognised as its own condition, and its symptomatic overlap with other conditions, such as borderline personality disorder, means that it's thought to be widely underdiagnosed. Perhaps it's something to do with the fact that it is a definitively complex, confusing condition (again, the clue is in the name) that makes people, especially objective medicine, so unaware and afraid of it.

Mental illness as a whole has become largely destigmatised in the last decade, something vital and welcomed by those who experience issues with their mental health. Up until recently, depression and anxiety were deemed too taboo to talk about, and in many areas of society this taboo still exists. However, the mainstream media has made it more commonplace and acceptable to discuss those mental illnesses deemed to be less outwardly 'scary', telling people such things as 'it's OK to feel sad' or 'it's OK to be anxious about the doomed world'. Whilst this may indeed be normal, is it so 'OK'? We're told that it's 'OK' if we're down or anxious – yet, more often than not, there is no substantive support provided. If it's so OK to talk about it, then why did suicides rise by 10 per cent in 2018?

In the winter of 2015, my mind started becoming grey again. I sought help from my new university NHS doctors, and they put me on the waiting list for general talking therapy. I attended an assessment in a church basement and offloaded my troubles to the assessor. She appeared somewhat overwhelmed, as therapists often are with me. She told me she wasn't sure they had the right services for my problems, but that she would put me on the list anyway and see what came up after she referred me. That was December 2015. I didn't begin my talking therapy until February 2017 - a fourteen-month wait, interspersed with varying bouts of suicidality. Six months or so into this wait, I was called by another assessor to check in on me. It was summertime and I walked down my parents' garden path, trying to convey to this face-less stranger how much I needed help. Unless you give the impression you're going to kill yourself within the next hour, you'll have to wait an undisclosed number of months (and even when imminently suicidal, you'll probably still have to wait). Prevention is shadowed by last-minute intervention.

The last decade of Tory-led austerity in the UK has meant that mental-health services have been cut drasti-cally. A report by Trade Union Congress in 2018 found that between 2013 and 2018, the number of patients per one mental-health doctor rose from 186 to 253 patients, and the number of patients per one mental-health nurse rose from twenty-nine patients to thirty-nine patients. This shortage in staff has led to a major crisis. The NHS is supposed to offer non-urgent treatments, including treatments for mental-health conditions, within eighteen weeks of the initial referral. According to the Royal College of Psychiatry, in 2020, these waiting lists usually ranged anywhere from four weeks to over six months. After this initial waiting time, the RCS found that those with severe mental illnesses (including bipolar and PTSD) waited up to two years for substantial treatment, whilst those with conditions including depression and anxiety could wait up to four years.

The government's budget in 2018 proposed to increase mental-health funding in a five-year plan in 2018. However, the Health Foundation has stated that these budgets aren't enough to stop this current crisis. They propose that at least an extra £1.5 billion would be needed to substantially improve these services. Upon the writing of this book, we still don't know the further impact on mental-health crises due to the ongoing Covid-19 pandemic. It's safe to assume that the hardships our society has faced in the pandemic, compounded by the chaotic handling of it by our government, will only increase the urgent need for substantial mental-health support services.

It might indeed be OK and even lifesaving to express our depressed, anxious or traumatised selves with our loved ones, but it's not OK that we are led to such illnesses or conditions through a sick society and it's not OK that we're usually left alone to try and find our way through it. Sure, it's OK to feel blue because everyone else feels those murky depths too. It's vital to express our pain and hurt, as suppressing those emotions can harm us even further. But it's not OK that misogyny, racism, capitalism, transphobia and ableism have left our body-minds in this painful mess. We must ask how many employers truly accept their employee's depression and allow them time off when they are going through a particularly difficult episode. How many people are still expected to 'just get on with it', even after they've tried to talk about it?

Another problem with the current public discourse on mental health is that only certain acceptable, palatable aspects of mental illnesses have even begun to be destigmatised. This palatable discussion of mental illness in the mainstream has led to the avoidance of the uglier, disastrous side of mental illness. What wider society can't currently seem to confront is the harder conversations. We're not outwardly talking about making yourself vomit after every meal because it's the only way to release the pain and anger you feel deep inside. We aren't talking about dermatophagia, the act of compulsively biting the skin on one's fingers as a nervous tick, or trichotillomania, pulling one's hair out compulsively. We aren't talking about the eruptive anger we can feel in the throes of a breakdown, the threats we might make to strangers or loved ones. We aren't substantially talking about suicide, of wanting to die because you simply don't care about being alive any more because you can't bear to wake up tomorrow to the same old repetitive shit. We aren't talking about the physical effects of failed suicide attempts. We aren't talking about breaking down in the middle of the street and screaming at passers-by. And if we are talking about all of these things, we're instead talking about how crazy, scary and unstable the people are who experience them.

These aspects of mental illness aren't as attractive, aren't as Instagrammable. I am guilty of this myself, of beautifying my mental illness. When I post on Instagram, trying to raise awareness of the difficulties of living with an unstable, traumatic condition, I mediate it with beauty. I choose an appropriate photograph to go alongside it: I will look sad and pale, but I will still look beautiful, just the right angle so people still think I'm hot. Or I will think I look actively beautiful, and I will use it as a chance to subvert the assumptions such a photograph may evoke. I don't post pictures of my trauma responses, such as my chewed-up, bleeding thumb after a trigger has set me off to mindlessly hurt myself. I don't post pictures of myself doing class-A drugs in a bathroom alone at a party that I am too anxious to socialise at without them. When will we start honestly talking about these more secret sides of mental illness, and even more importantly, when will we start being able to listen?

These silent sides of trauma and mental illness further invoke the feelings of shame we already feel. This silent shame becomes a vicious cycle – we're ashamed of our experiences of sexual violence, so we resort to trauma responses such as those I've listed above; we're ashamed of these trauma responses due to the societal stigma attached to them, so we remain silent, and the shame grows larger and larger. Sometimes, the weight of that shame becomes too heavy a burden to live with at all.

We don't all survive sexual violence. But there's nuance to this conversation, too. You can be both a victim and a survivor, even if you don't ultimately survive. As Lachrista Greco (@theguerrillafeminist) says, even if a survivor has ultimately passed away, they're still a survivor – just because they took their own life doesn't mean we have to take away their label of survivor. During the writing of this book, on 4 August 2020, Daisy Coleman died by taking her own life. Daisy was the survivor at the centre of the 2012 Maryville rape case. Daisy was raped at the age of fourteen at a frat party, but the accused was never convicted. Daisy, however, was convicted in the court of public opinion. From the age of fourteen until her death aged twenty-three, she was tormented both on- and offline. Her family was harassed and she lost her job. A Fox News guest taunted, 'What did she expect to happen at one in the morning after sneaking out?' Daisy attempted to take her own life in 2014, but after she survived the attempt, she co-founded the teen-led *SafeBAE*, an organisation dedicated to preventing sexual assault in high schools. She took part in the Netflix documentary *Audrie & Daisy*, which told Daisy's story alongside the story of Audrie Pott. Audrie Pott was sexually assaulted by three boys in 2012 and she took her own life eight days later. Daisy Coleman called herself a survivor, and she is still a survivor. Even if she decided to end the pain eventually, that doesn't take away from the fact that she had persisted for so long. She was tenacious and resilient, as so many survivors have to be. Daisy Coleman's death tragically radiated out, too. Four months after Daisy's death, her mother Melinda, who'd tenaciously supported and defended her daughter, took her own life too. Sexual violence doesn't just involve two people; more often than not, the lives of those closest to survivor-victims are irrevocably damaged too.

When I was fifteen, I was suicidal. I would think of jumping out of windows, think of running to train tracks, dream of slitting my wrists to end it all. When I was eighteen, I was depressed, dealing with the fallout of my childhood abuse and a recent break-up with my childhood sweetheart. I had a fight with one of my best friends and took an overdose of my antidepressants. My friend found me and made me throw up the pills. I don't think the number of pills I took had any real capacity to damage me, but the intent was there. I'd taken the furthest step in actualising my suicidal ideation yet. It terrified me. It still terrifies me. The other night I had a dream that I was deeply suicidal again. I was waiting for someone in my dream that I knew would never come. I waited on a doorstep and decided that it was finally time to take my own life. I woke up jarred. These feelings had been dormant for so long. Could they be ready to re-emerge at any moment? I spent the following day in a haze and went to bed at 5 p.m., too afraid that the world could sink me down again, that the grey could return so unbelievably quickly.

It's not even sad or tragic in my head, this urge to die. It just is; it's a desire, an urge, like wanting to get a pastry from the shop or to go swimming this weekend. I'm not thinking of others or of myself, I just want to die and that's it. It is not beautiful or poetic. I know with certainty that I will be suicidal again in my life. Probably seriously so. This is not simply negative thinking, but rather, realistic thinking. I have drifted in and out of suicidality since I was fifteen. As quickly as the storm comes, so too it passes. My therapist asks me the last time I was seriously suicidal, and I realise it wasn't even a year ago. I can want to die one evening and forget about it the next morning. The doctors ask me how often my mood changes and I tell them I do not know. It could be within an hour, a minute, a week, a drink, a song, a text. The world turns to empty grey for a week, and the sun comes out just days later. It is tiring and it is terrifying, but I try my hardest to be comforted by how rapidly things can return to being OK.

The world may feel subdued, hazy; it will feel like

the world is a movie slightly out of sync, lips moving but the words coming out too slow. But it will soon return to my normal. I get intrusive thoughts; thoughts of stabbing my arms and thighs, of slitting my throat. Things will not always be this bad. And then they will be again. And then they will get better again. It's tiring and sometimes the cycle seems pointless. Nonetheless, we persist. We keep going. I have the word 'golden' tattooed in my own script on my inner right forearm. When people ask me why I have it, I tell them it's because golden hour is my favourite time of the day. I let them believe that I'm a cheesy, typical millennial indie girl. The real reason, which I often skim over for ease and privacy, is to remind myself of the morning, because my darkest points usually come late at night. In the depths of winter, the depths of night, my psyche sinks to its lowest. My insides feel as black as the cold outside my window, and I can't possibly see how I can make it to tomorrow. I force myself to think of the golden morning dawn. I force myself to keep going just to see one last morning, to see the purity of the sun as it erupts from the horizon one last time. Every single time, I fall asleep before the sun rises. The idea of it keeps me alive, keeps me breathing until that next day. I sleep through the idea that keeps me alive and repeat this ritual endlessly. I may rarely see this so beloved sunrise of mine, but the fact it is always there, relentlessly, unconditionally, has kept me alive through so many dark nights.

C-PTSD is a messy condition that ebbs and flows throughout my life. It is a life of contradiction; I become preoccupied with my abusers but also try to repress what occurred; I can be afraid of men and sex but seek out dangerous sexual situations, in an attempt to 'relive' or 'reclaim' my abusive past. It can be very ugly.

One day, I'm triggered. My head feels heavy. My limbs become numb. I've been in a depressive episode this week – I'm having to suddenly move house, go through a relationship crisis and have my wisdom tooth out under sedation. It's been a tough few days. One morning, on my first day back at work since my dental surgery, my rapist's friend is at my bus stop. Incidentally, this friend of his looks a lot like him. I'm originally triggered by his likeness to David. This happens when I see men with a certain hairstyle and certain accessories. I quickly turn my face away and try to pretend that this lookalike isn't there. Then he gets on the same bus as me – something unsurprising, seeing as only three buses stop at my stop and they all go in the same direction. He comes up the stairs of the double-decker bus behind me and as I sit down, I get to see him pass me, heading toward the back of the bus. I'm suddenly certain that it actually is one of David's friends. I'm not completely sure, but something inside me makes me feel sure I'm correct. This man was a friend I'd been told had excommunicated David. I'd never actually met this friend before, so my fixation and panic make me feel crazy, obsessed. He looks at me . . . Does he know me? Can he place me? Does he remember what his friend did to me? That I am the victim, the girl who caused 'all those issues' a few years ago? Does he actually look at me, or am I creating a narrative in my head of a guilt-struck near-stranger on a rush-hour bus? As I get off at my stop, I try to search for him, to confirm it's him in the faces of the packed top deck. I can't find him - I've failed.

On the evening of the bus-ride incident, I don't feel like my hands are mine. My mind feels clouded, like he has shrouded it for the countless time. I feel like I'm sewn to the back of my body, one step removed, like Peter Pan and his shadow. I scramble to find the stable sense of me. The loneliness is excruciating. I tell myself it's stupid, I'm stupid, it's all my fault. I made up the man on the bus, he was just a stranger. You made all this up and they all know it. You are a liar, a fraud, a thief of pain. I feel empty, numb, lifeless.

The bus incident reminds me that David and I still live in a physical proximity to one another. It reminds me of what my body always knows, that he could still be near, still be a danger. That I could get on the same bus as *him*, not his friend. I once saw another friend of his crossing the road at the same pedestrian crossing as me whilst leaving my therapy appointment. This friend, whose identity I was sure of that time, looked straight through me. I didn't exist – in his small world I was another stranger on a busy London road. Two degrees of separation; maybe next time it will actually be him.

When I see men who look like David, it's like being stabbed in the abdomen. I have to reassure myself: not all people wearing glasses are you. Not all people are you. On buses, on trains, on tubes, on streets. All people could be him. They catch my eye. Do they see the fear in my face? Do they see the faltering recognition; the terror that you could be coming towards me? A knife in your hands ready to slice me in two once more. House keys as tiny knives in my own hand, ready to fight back this time. But you've been ordered to stay away from me, so you probably would. Three years later, and there are fewer men who look like David. Has the style of the millennial man changed, or have I begun to heal? I can go to London Bridge without the fear he will be at the bottom of every escalator. I can walk down the street, holding hands with my partner, knowing I am safe, if just for a moment.

Another day, a year after the bus incident above, I am in the park next to my house in the middle of a June heatwave. The air is thick and dry, the park buzzing with people who have just emerged from their houses after a day of working from home during the Covid-19 pandemic. I sit on a striped towel and read in the still-strong evening sun. There are children playing, running with hoops. There is a mother and daughter sunbathing in front of me, the daughter a wheelchair user. I see a man approaching, not directly towards me but to the hill I am sitting on. He is middle-aged and tanned like leather, his greying hair falls to his shoulder in loose waves. He looks enough like the man who assaulted me in Australia for my body to go into overdrive; tense, my hairs standing on end, heart beating faster and harder. He doesn't even acknowledge me. He sits a few metres away and begins to do sit-ups. I feel his breathing on me. I doubt he even registers my existence. I feel like he is watching me; I turn around too many times to see that he hasn't glanced my way. This is how it feels to be triggered. You sit, minding your own business, thinking of the benign worries of that day, the sweat dripping down from behind your knees, ruminating on the intense chapter on suicide prevention in the transformative justice anthology you're reading – and then your body gets dragged back to five years ago, lying on that beach in the equally blaring sunshine. I can see that I am in a park in South London, I see my striped towel and the old gym shorts I am wearing. Yet my flesh and my nerves feel struck, my neurons firing to get away, to stay safe as he has returned. I try to stick it out, try to punish my body-mind to overcome, convincing myself that the feelings will pass. They do not pass. I keep turning around – do I look crazy, paranoid? The words on the page I read become fuzzy, as hot as the air around me. I finally give myself some peace. I get up, walk further up the hill towards my home. I get home and have a weak beer, watching *Queer Eye* until I forget about the man in the park. I tell my friends I want to speak to them, and then I decide to ignore them. I fall asleep. There is no resounding hope at the end of this day; it just ends.

The depression and dissociation come like the start of a film. Like being in the cinema before the film begins, the sound bringing your attention to the supersonic speakers they have surrounding you. It pulls my body from my skin, booming, moving around like those little balls of metal you see bouncing off the sub-woofers. When I want to hurt myself, the wanting comes in waves, just like those soundwaves. More aptly, it comes in cataclysms, typhoons. It comes to me when I look out of the window and see grey. I feel myself leave and need to stab myself to return. I feel myself pull my hair out of its follicles and the memories flood in their place.

Despite the hellishness of these moments, I don't want to be cured of my trauma. I don't think it's possible. I will never completely get over it, will never be absolutely 'cured'. I will forever be weaving in and out of sanity, reality and happiness, forever be weaving in and out of insanity, derealisation and melancholy. Assuredly, things get better. And then they get worse. And then they get better. I am not a failure for the struggle I have in getting through some days, nor am I a failure for oscillating between sheer happiness and the numbing depths of depression. I am both a survivor and a victim, oscillating forever between well and unwell – and that is OK.

In the darkest moments, I tell myself that I will get up in the morning and make some tea with oat milk. I'll listen to that new album by an old favourite. I'll let his melodies ripple through me: saxophones, brass of calm, reminding myself that I've survived this in the past and I will survive it once more. I will find them again; the love and the pull, the beautiful pull of life. It is OK to be sad right now, you have enough to mourn. I will stay alive tonight, so that I can smell my new perfume tomorrow. Today I wear bergamot. Tomorrow, I will wear jasmine. Choosing a bouquet in place of the wreath I once dreamed of.

# Chapter 7

# What Our Bodies Tell Us

The historical and contemporary story of modern illness is long entwined with trauma and surviving adverse experiences, and has been recounted in such works as *The Body Keeps the Score* and the popular TED talk with the paediatrician Nadine Burke Harris. Early childhood trauma, and trauma later in life, triples the risk of heart and lung disease and decreases life expectancy by twenty years. This trauma is not exclusively related to sexual abuse, but also to other types of physical abuse, emotional abuse, living with a parent with a mental illness, and living in poverty.

In the mid-1990s, a groundbreaking study was done on Adverse Childhood Experiences (ACEs) that looked at the effects of these ACEs on now-grown adults. ACEs are defined as being any of the following: domestic violence; parental abandonment through separation or divorce; a parent with a mental-health condition; being the victim of abuse (physical, sexual and/or emotional); being the victim of neglect (physical and emotional); a member of the household being in prison; growing up in a household in which there are adults experiencing alcohol- and drug-use problems. The study correlated ACE scores; you would get a 'point' for each adverse experience you had lived through as a child. The study found that ACEs were extremely common, with 67 per cent of participants experiencing at least one and 12.6 per cent having four or more. They also found an upsetting correlation: the higher your ACE score, the worse your health outcome. For someone with an ACE score of four or more, depression was four and a half times more likely than someone without these experiences. Suicidality was twelve times more likely. A person with an ACE score of seven or more had triple the lifetime risk of lung cancer and three and a half times the risk of ischemic heart disease.

Research found two key reasons for this. The first one is expected and may be used as a retort against notions of empathy for these struggling people: higher ACEs mean a higher likelihood of engaging in risky coping behaviours such as drinking, smoking and taking drugs. In response to unsympathetic cynics, Nadine Burke-Harris and the field of trauma studies as a whole can respond that early adversity and trauma

affects areas like the nucleus accumbens, the pleasure and reward centre of the brain that is implicated in substance dependence. It inhibits the prefrontal cortex, which is necessary for impulse control and executive function, a critical area for learning. On MRI scans, we see measurable differences in the amygdala, the brain's fear response centre. So, there are known neurological reasons why folks exposed to high doses of adversity are more likely to engage in high-risk behaviour.

Yet even if they don't engage in high-risk behaviour, survivors of adverse childhood experiences still have a higher risk for the above health problems. This is because of the brain and body's stress-response system that governs our fight-or-flight response. When we're stressed, our bodies release the hormones adrenaline and cortisol to protect us. This is great for immediate, temporary threats. However, when that threat is repeated − for example, with abuse, or the threat of abuse, occurring frequently − our stress systems go into overdrive and often damage our health. These effects of trauma affect brain structure and function, our immune system, hormonal systems and our DNA.

I explain all this to exemplify the profound physical effects frequently caused by traumatic experiences. Children are more affected by such trauma, due to their developing brains and their different ways of processing information. They are developing their sense of self and their core beliefs about how the world around them works. When actions or words tell them repeatedly that they're not loved or that they're somehow 'wrong', they eventually begin to believe it and take it on as their identity. However, trauma at any time in our life can send our body into overdrive, as I discussed in the prior chapter.

Our bodies and our minds are inextricably entwined, they're our body-minds. What occurs in our consciousness, or in our unconsciousness if we were harmed whilst in that state (for example, in our sleep), has a constant, interdependent relationship with our physical bodies. People with adverse experiences are more likely to be physically or mentally ill, and women are more likely to become chronically ill too. Therefore it follows that women and feminised people with adverse experiences are at a very high risk of developing long-term health problems. Women generally are at higher risk for heart disease, autoimmune diseases and chronic pain conditions. Multiple studies have shown that those who survive childhood sexual abuse are more likely to develop chronic pelvic pain and inflammatory conditions. There's a correlation between those who are survivors of sexual violence and those who have vaginismus and ovarian cysts. Sexual-abuse survivors are more likely to develop fibromyalgia, with rape survivors being three times more likely than the general population to develop fibromyalgia. The common conception is that sexual trauma causes intense, ongoing emotional pain – but these statistics and our lived realities show that it can cause physical pain too.

Women, and in particular traumatised women, have a long and fraught relationship with pain and illness. Sick women in Western medicine were originally diagnosed with hysteria in Ancient Greek times, *hystera* meaning womb, with the source of the condition being a wandering womb. What would these Ancient Greeks say about endometriosis, artist Johanna Hedva asks. About a millennium later, in medieval times, the source of our sickness was demonic possession. In the 1700s, hysteria became grouped in with other 'nervous disorders'. *Verywell Mind* tells me that the symptoms of hysteria included: nervousness, hallucinations, paralysis, fainting, insomnia, sexual forwardness and irritability. Many of us in the present day would have easily been diagnosed with the condition. At this time, there was excitable discussion over whether it was caused by gynaecological or neurological problems.

Then, Freud came on the scene in the late 1800s. The 'father of modern psychology', Freud initially theorised that women's hysterical symptoms came from repressed memories of childhood sexual abuse that then material-ised in physical symptoms. It was quickly realised that if this theory was correct, then in saying that women and girls were being abused, there must be people doing the abusing, implicating the fathers, uncles, grand-fathers and other men in society. It was thus deter-mined that the theory must be changed – clearly such abuse couldn't possibly be taking place. Revising his research, Freud claimed it was actually only imagined abuse that happened; repressed false memories ignited by repressed penis-envying fantasies. Freud deduced that psychoanalysis would be the cure for these lying, hysterical women. Women were now categorised as only believing they were physically ill because of their repressed mental illness. Medicine has since clung onto this idea that if a medically objective, testable cause cannot be found for a person's illness, then the sickness must be caused by the unconscious mind. It became the institutionalised norm to not trust women and people with feminized bodies, such as trans and gender-non-conforming people, when they speak of their own bodies.

Hysteria did not disappear, but was dissolved into multiple new labels, many of which have since been established by 'objective' biomedicine; for example, in cases of epilepsy and multiple sclerosis. It's thought that 'Anna O', one of the key female patients used in Sigmund Freud's studies on hysteria, actually had neurologically caused temporal-lobe epilepsy rather than hysteria or any other psychiatric disorder. The symptoms occurring in hysteria and other such nervous disorders were labelled as psychogenic or psychosomatic – that is, caused by the mind. Over the decades, hysteria became Briquet's syndrome, which then became somatic disorder and conversion disorder. We also have c-PTSD, dissociative identity disorder, borderline personality disorder, chronic pain conditions, fibromyalgia and chronic fatigue syndrome (also known as myalgic encephalomyelitis or ME). I am not saying that these latter conditions do not exist and do not cause immense struggles throughout our lives – I myself live with some of these conditions – but I do believe that in many ways, hysteria has simply morphed into new medicalised forms. The medical terms may change, but the dismissal of women remains a constant in the medical landscape. Will we look back in a century's time at the labelling and dismissal of such modern patients in a similar way to the way in which we look back at the diagnosis of hysteria now?

It would be all well and good if these newer diagnostic labels meant we got more help and that more research was going towards ways to alleviate the pain caused by them, but that is far from the case. According to the Chronic Pain Research Alliance, research into chronic pain conditions is significantly underfunded in relation to how many people experience them and how debilitating they can be, with the National Institute of Health in the USA investing only $1.06 per affected person, in comparison to $35 per person with diabetes. Similarly, recent funding secured for pain research by Versus Arthritis UK invests an overall average of 86p per chronic-pain patient (of which there are 28 million in the UK). The UK government's contribution to that research amounts to an investment of only 43p per person. And that's just for the conditions that are, albeit often controversially, accepted by the medical community. There are plenty of people left wandering without hope, living with medically undiagnosed mysteries.

The trouble is, the terms 'psychogenic' or 'psychosomatic' often translate to 'not real' in the eyes of many medical practitioners. With medically contested conditions such as fibromyalgia and the like, there's a common split between cynical doctors and their tenacious patients. Many doctors believe that the illness is 'all in their heads', a kind of conversion occurring between their emotional trauma and its physical expression. Patients and critical feminist scholars respond that it's not 'just in our heads' – that these women have physical illnesses that must have a root organic cause. They want to make clear that these women aren't pathologically crazy. They tell us that it's not our minds but our bodies that are in trouble. Rationalist Western society has taught us this binary: it's either your body or your mind that's causing the pain. What if it's both? What if, as I believe in my own case, the traumas I experienced are at the root of my all-too-real physical symptoms? As Carolyn Lazard writes, 'pain is the body calling out for attention', and it seems clear that we need to start paying attention. Even if their root is psychological, it doesn't mean that the pain and the other symptoms are illusions.

Elaine Scarry says that pain is 'language destroying', and many other theorists and writers of pain also claim that it's essentially incommunicable. Incidentally, during a traumatic experience, the areas of our brain that process and construct language shut down. So, trauma is pre-verbal, pre-lingual and pre-discursive. Trauma, like pain, is rooted in the body first before it is constructed into language. It is inherently felt before it can ever be uttered. We may be able to translate our experiences, our pain or our trauma as best we can into the written or spoken word, but there will forever be an inexpressible part. It becomes exhausting telling people about pain, embodying it fully to explain the intricacies and agonies. We have to do it often - to our doctors, to institutions, to our loved ones. I'm in pain most of the time, and I keep it to myself, or else I'd be constantly expressing the hurt. I would be boring; perhaps I have already become boring. I wish I never had to explain my pain to anyone again, but there we are.

Women and feminised people have long been seen as pathological, told that their physical symptoms are psychogenic. Whether or not the root of an illness is caused by the physical or the mental, any mental or emotional roots of very physical pains are so often dismissed. They're seen as made up, constructed, converted. As I write this, my best friend, who also lives with chronic pain, sends me a meme from Twitter user @sicc_bitch. It goes:

PATIENT: Hello, I am in a lot of pain all the time.
DOCTOR: Hmm. Are you just saying that to get attention?
PATIENT: Yes. Medical attention.

We laugh, but this is the brutal reality of it. Women and feminised people are dismissed because we're definitively emotional. We're told it's all in our heads, the roots of masculine, rationalist thought seeping through to our everyday. What these rationalists seem to forget is that everything we experience is 'all in our heads'. In my worries about my pain and peripheral numbness, I admitted to my doctor friend that I was worried it was 'all in my head'. Her response, quite helpfully, was to explain that, by definition, all pain is in our heads. Pain is only pain because our nerves send signals to our brain telling us that something's wrong. Even if it were 'all in our heads' the way the doubters insinuate, what would be so farcical about that? Pain is still pain, even if there is no clear physical source. The webs of doubt seep through once more, blaming the victim in cases of chronic illness as well as sexual violence. Just as the survivor–victim is dismissed, so too often is the feminised medical patient.

At the start of this chapter, I gave an overview of the way our bodies can be affected when our minds stay in an overactivated state post-trauma. Our bodies go into overdrive to protect ourselves, and, accordingly, parts of our bodies are neglected – organs, muscles. When we're triggered and we freeze, parts of our internal bodies can freeze too. The longer this goes on for, unnoticed or untreated, the worse the physical effects can be. As Lucia Osborne-Crowley writes in *I Choose Elena*, 'The patient faces a future defined by illness as penance for being unable to escape the unbearable past.'

★

During the first draft of this book, I was in the process of getting a diagnosis for fibromyalgia. Fibromyalgia syndrome is a chronic pain disorder, characterised by widespread multisite pain, fatigue, difficulty concentrating (known as brain or fibro-fog) and a myriad of other symptoms dependent on each person. The truth is, researchers don't know that much about the condition. There seems to be an endless number of theories. It is currently thought that in fibromyalgia, the brain and nervous system misinterpret or overreact to pain signals. Some studies have shown that traumatic abuse injures the brain in certain ways that may cause the symptoms of fibromyalgia, whilst other studies have proposed that fibromyalgia may be linked to certain microbes in the gut. It's thought that it can be triggered by stress, trauma, genes and/or infections.

The symptoms: the pain, the fatigue and the seemingly infinite number of other symptoms people diagnosed with fibromyalgia suffer with are indeed very real things. What I doubt, however, is that fibromyalgia is a whole diagnosis on its own. Paul Ingraham, a pain specialist who himself has been diagnosed with fibromyalgia, argues, 'Fibromyalgia is not an explanatory diagnosis. It sheds no light on the nature of the beast; it's just a label for a distinctive but unexplained pattern of symptoms.' Biomedicine doesn't, and can likely never, know everything about the human body and its various states. There are a multitude of undiagnosed, undiscovered conditions people will be living with – especially those that women and people with female sex traits experience in supposed 'mystery'.

As Maya Dusenbery writes about in *Doing Harm*, many women are diagnosed with 'medically undiagnosed conditions' when their symptoms seemingly have no cause. Fibromyalgia often seems to just be a medicalised branch for these 'medically undiagnosed' mysteries. There is no objective medical test for fibromyalgia. Symptoms of the disorder cannot currently be proven with blood tests, imaging machines or biopsies. There is the tender points test, where the doctor will press on certain points of your body to see if they can reproduce the pain, and if you have a certain number of these tender points, they diagnose you with fibromyalgia. However, this test isn't used everywhere, and has recently been changed to a more general test for multisite pain. Fibromyalgia is essentially the diagnosis given when they've run out of other options. Hypothetically, this could be OK. Science and medicine do not and cannot ever know absolutely everything about our bodies and the world around us. The problem, however, is that the diagnosis of fibromyalgia seems to be where most attention to the condition ends. There's a split in the medical community regarding fibromyalgia. It's like the aforementioned split between the cynical doctor and the tenacious patient. Essentially, one half of medicine thinks it exists as a physical disease, whilst the other half doesn't and suggests that mental and emotional states play the biggest role. Due to the dominance of medical authority in our culture, those who suffer from the symptoms of fibromyalgia are left in what Kristin Barker, writer of *The Fibromyalgia Story*, calls 'epistemological purgatory': we feel these symptoms so acutely within ourselves, yet no medical authority can explicitly confirm our inner turmoil.

The condition is as cultural as it is physical. Chronic pain generally, and fibromyalgia specifically, have both physical and social effects. We are disbelieved by doctors and by the general public. There's a 'double disruption', as Leslie Cooper theorised – the existence of the condition itself and then the medical and cultural doubt that the illness is even real. This 'double disruption' often leads to depression and suicidality in those diagnosed with fibromyalgia – rates of self-harm in rheumatological conditions are highest amongst fibromyalgia patients. For many people, though, despite the cultural repercussions of the diagnostic label of fibromyalgia, it's still worth it to just have a name for the pain and fatigue you're living with every day. Even if that diagnosis is contested, it's still something you can point to. It's still a tool you can use to tell people that there's a designator for what you're experiencing, that you're not making it up and that other people have felt it too.

Through my voyage into the strange world of pain and fibromyalgia, I joined Facebook support groups for those experiencing the condition. I felt alienated, the usual members twice my age, with very different life experiences from my own. Following the tone of self-help books for the condition, they declare fibromyalgia 'a beast to be tackled', a beast that may have won frequently. Even the quote I used earlier refers to the condition as the 'beast'. They fight it, the big bad condition. What they usually fail to note is the common underlying cause of fibromyalgia and somatic pain: a deeply problematic world and the trauma it causes. The groups and best-selling books that propose to fix or help sufferers make the condition legendary. We are painted as mythical queens who must slay the dragon of fibromyalgia, when, in reality, we're people who've been physically damaged by an unequal society.

Ninety per cent of fibromyalgia patients are women, with the condition being more common in white women and specifically low-income white women. The theory for this demographic divide is that low-income white women are more likely to endure the causes of fibromyalgia – stress and trauma – whilst simultaneously having no cultural coping mechanisms for the pain. People in Western capitalist cultures, namely white women in regard to chronic pain, often believe that we are entitled to a pain-free life. We have been told that pain and suffering are abnormal and become 'impatient with the experience of pain, [so] we seek quick solutions to ensure our freedom from its grip', as Kristin Baker puts it. We don't often have the cultural mechanisms of community set up well enough to help us cope with this pain. So, we're led to crave medical confirmation. We crave external authority to be validated. We medicalise whatever we can, as it reinforces our reality. We medicalise trauma as PTSD, pain as fibromyalgia. This doesn't mean these things aren't real, but will relying on these structures solve our pain? And are we even entitled to freedom from pain? What is life without pain? If we reached utopia, dismantled rape culture and oppressive forces, would we be free of pain?

My thoughts around fibromyalgia as a diagnosis dramatically changed in a short amount of time. I sought the diagnosis; craved it. I endeavoured to label myself as I thought it would help. The main thing that had changed was the consensus from the doctors who agreed that I may have it. Was this new scepticism rooted in self-doubt? My own reaction of doubt simply mirrored how society views the condition. Most people don't know what it is, and if they do, they struggle to understand it as a real thing. Was I critical for the reasons I've given above or is there something more, some element of doubt and gaslighting that I betray myself with? There is something undeniably helpful in having a name for it. Even if it's not the right name, there is the relief; the need to not be seen as crazy, even if just by a few people. It might be another word for hysteria, it might be unknown, but at least there's a space for it. At least there's some community; fellow people who are left in the pain and fatigue that this mystery condition brings with it. Perhaps I prefer Amy Berkowitz's name for the condition that she coins in *Tender Points*: 'My Body is Haunted by a Certain Trauma'. Among many other translations, diagnoses can mean you are not alone, there are others like you. At least the mystery 'thing' can be a medically defined mystery now.

Ten months after being referred to a rheumatologist for suspected fibromyalgia, I ultimately had to turn to private healthcare. The pain was getting worse; I was incapacitated most days. After a couple of appointments with a rheumatologist and numerous tests, I was diagnosed with Hypermobile Spectrum Disorder (HSD), with specific joint instability in both my hips and my neck. I'd been waiting eight years for a doctor to take my pain seriously, and it took only two weeks for my new doctor to diagnose me with this chronic, disabling but manageable condition. He prescribed me physiotherapy and nerve blockers and referred me to an orthopaedic surgeon for further treatments.

I'd been led to believe for so long that I was crazy, that it was in my head, that it was just my depression. A month before this diagnosis of HSD, I was called up by a pharmacist at my doctor's surgery. The purpose of this call was to lecture me on pain medication and the fact that I should be doing more to combat my pain. As she patronized me and told me I needed to increase my antidepressants to deal with the pain, I began to cry. That day, I had barely been able to get out of my bed because my hips were so unstable and were causing so much pain. On the phone, I reeled off the ways I try to combat my pain: walking, yoga, over-the-counter medication, baths, Tiger Balm, massages, foam rollers. She was stunned at this and agreed that yes, I seemed to already be trying quite hard. Why was I only allowed sympathy once I'd declared how much of a 'good patient' I was? Why was I made to feel like a drug-seeker, a liar, for overreacting, just because I needed help with my debilitating pain?

I do believe the symptoms of fibromyalgia are real, yet I think doctors throw the term at people when they can't or won't find out the true cause of a patient's symptoms. I could have gone on for years, undiagnosed or misdiagnosed, and my actual condition would have progressed; wearing down my joints and teaching my body that pain was normal. I still won't know for another year or so whether the untreated pain I've been in for years has forever morphed into chronic pain. How much relief could have been found had I been truly listened to earlier? And, worst of all, I know that I'm lucky. I have the privilege of access to private healthcare through my parents' work policy. What of the millions in this country who don't have this privilege? What of all those who remain victims of the underfunded and overstretched NHS? When the medical world tells you there's nothing wrong, you internalise that. I was trying to be a detectorist for my own condition, but how could I think I'd find anything when the doctors wouldn't help?

What comes with my condition, my pain or whatever we will call it on a given day, is the looming spectre of impostor syndrome. Yet another syndrome – a syndrome of a syndrome of a syndrome. An impostor on pain - the worst kind of intrusion one could make. I tell myself that my pain isn't enough, it mustn't be as bad as others', so my warped logic leads me to the conclusion that I must be making it up. I read and study medical patriarchy, the inherent misogyny of the medical industry, and though I should be soothed by the recognition of medical gaslighting and the inaccuracy of medical practitioners when it comes to feminised pain, I find myself falling further into the hole of self-doubt. Maybe I am a hypochondriac, or worse, its etymologically feminine opposite: hysterical. This is another, unwritten, symptom of any chronic, culturally and medically contested illness.

Maybe if it was worse, I'd know; and even more, if it was worse, *they* (the doctors, society) would know. I feel guilt for being able to stay in bed. I feel sick with it, sick with the sickness. Sick with not being able to be as productive as capitalism tells me I should be. I try to take a day off and find myself doing my taxes instead. I try to finish writing at 7 p.m. and watch TV to relax, but continue filling my brain with news articles, Instagram posts for someone's life-saving fundraisers, Twitter threads on abusive men. There's a certain special routine of doubt and guilt reserved for those who live with chronic illness. Chronic illness can be seen as biographical disruption – some days you're fine, your 'normal' baseline self; other days your life halts, you become a ghost, you're not who you seemed to be. I wake up and don't feel too fatigued, go to work and meet a friend for coffee, or have a two-hour long Zoom reading group. I make myself dinner and stay up reading until midnight. I'm fine. Then, the next day I'm incapacitated. Temporarily blinded by a migraine or struggling to stand because of my hip pain. This pendulum nature of our days leaves plenty of room for the webs of doubt to seep through in the liminal spaces.

In line with what Maya Dusenbery explains in *Doing Harm*, I fall into the double bind of the woman in pain: I'm either hysterical, overreacting and seeking attention for something that can't be that painful; or I'm so calm and collected, a calmness I only perform so that the doctor may deem me 'sane' and, believe me, that I can't be as unwell as I say. It seems this bind goes further than the doctor's office. I internalise this to my own body. If I'm truly expressing my physical pain, I'll think I'm making it up – being dramatic or lazy. Or, if I'm grinning and bearing it, I'll tell myself it can't really be that bad. By the world or by ourselves, we risk being yellow-wallpapered, overpathologised as a hysterical woman in fake pain. Or we risk being gaslit, being told we're fine and that nothing is really wrong.

Like so much in this book and in life, the fact of surviving sexual violence interlinks with most things. Like sickness and disability, impostor syndrome creeps into feelings around survival too. In both cases, you are doubted by those around you and arrive at a place of self-doubt. You blame yourself: for not exercising enough, for inviting him back to your place. You doubt your own experiences because society is unremittingly woven into your individual life. Your own bodily reality is called into question – is it real? Am I making it up? Does this happen to everyone else too and I'm just making a big deal out of it? Traces of illness and violence can both be supposedly proven or disproven by institutional authorities. If your bloods come back with a biological marker, or if your rape kit finds evidence of an intruder, then you're partially safe. If nothing can be found? 'I'm sorry, there's not much we can do to help you.' The medical gaze pervades both of these institutions; if they can see into your body, see that you're telling the truth, then maybe you'll be believed. If not, there's nothing wrong, nothing happened, so get over it. But we shouldn't have to get over it. We're not impostors in either world. If we're in pain, we're in pain. If we're traumatised, we're traumatised. It's only when these simple facts can be accepted that we'll finally be able to move along in life with the pain and the harm beside us.

★

Around the same time as my musculoskeletal pain emerged, I developed the terrible blight of migraines. I remember the first attack clearly: I was in Year 10 and had been at a friend's house the night before for a Chinese takeaway. During the morning's English lesson, I had the most intense aura (the visual disturbance that comes with migraines). My vision tunnelled, everything circling down to a blurred hole in the centre of my vision. Trying to maintain normality, not wanting to cause a fuss but still not being able to see properly, I fumbled my way to the cafeteria with my friends at break-time. We ate the terrible KFC-style chicken baps that were all the rage in my high school. Then, things started getting worse. Along with the still-tunnelled vision, a brutal headache had begun behind my right eye – the eye still most often affected during my attacks – and I felt extremely nauseous. All I was certain of was that I needed darkness and I needed quiet. My friend took me to the sick bay and the nurse seemed worried. The school was on high alert as, only a few years before, a girl with similar symptoms who had dramatically worsened at school had tragically died from a brain tumour – and they gave me exactly what I needed. In the dark room I could see spots and flashing lights in my vision. This aura brought up the chicken bap I'd eaten only minutes earlier. My mum collected me and took me back to my poorly darkened room, where I lay for a few hours. This was the first time I developed the trusty jumper-over-the-eyes technique I still use to this day. Sleep warded it off, and I woke up with the needle behind my head mostly having disappeared, though its imprint lasted for a day afterwards.

My mum, after reading a few articles, suggested it could have been caused by MSG (a salt) added to the Chinese food I'd eaten the evening before. This controversial and still debated cause or occidental myth became the story of my migraine. Yet, despite avoiding certain foods, the migraines still plagued me.

In the years that followed, such migraine attacks became a common ordeal. They first came every couple of months, but now I can count on a buffet of headaches every month.

Alongside the more intense attacks, which come about twice a month, I've also developed chronic underlying headaches, rearing their head a few times a week. Pain begets pain: if my widespread pain is bad, or I'm struggling with my mental illness, the migraines come more frequently and more acutely. Intense attacks can last anything from four hours, twelve hours, up to thirty-six hours. They've become longer, more aggressive, and sleep often does little to combat them now. I just have to wait them out. People who don't have migraines struggle to comprehend the true nature of them. They aren't just a 'bad headache'. For me, my migraine may often first present as a 'bad headache', but this can't portray the torture they can become. Have you ever been to a food market and seen a cheesemonger pull out a tube of cheese with a cheese corer? Well, my brain is the cheese and the migraine attack is the corer. It's a precise cylinder behind my right eye that feels like it's being yanked out, or maybe frozen off. My vision begins to blur. It becomes hard to keep my eyes open at all. My neck seizes up, pain trailing down into my arms, and I begin to feel nausea wash over my whole body before I find the nearest toilet. All I can do is lie down, close my eyes, and wait for it to pass. My whole body shuts down for a day. The cruellest side-effect of a migraine attack for me is the incapacity to read. The greatest love of my life is reading. Books, the news, anything that feeds me more information to better understand life. Yet, when a migraine strikes, the long words I so desire become nonsensical in their blurred, noisy blocks. Every movement my eye tries to make along the sentence becomes a jackhammer that intensifies the migraine. I try to listen to podcasts instead, to give in to the non-visual, yet any information feels like screeching white noise mixed with nails on a chalk board. It must be dark, and it must be quiet. Quite often, it gets lonely. The isolation compounds and extends. The feeling post-migraine is like a hangover; the imprint of the drill is still there, a crater. Words come slower; your neck still feels too stiff to turn. You remember the hours of incapacitation yet strive to avoid the memory of it like an embarrassing mishap.

Rather than a mostly benign food additive, stress and trauma seem to be what triggers my brain's temporary shutdown. I was prescribed triptans, the most popular migraine medication. This medication mostly worked if I managed to take it in time, when the attack first began. The medication had side-effects whereby my face seized up and my jaw became fizzy with biological confusion. I would have been able to cope with these side-effects in exchange for freedom from the pain, but ultimately, I ended up having an allergic reaction (thanks, body). The attacks strike most frequently when I'm stressed or when I drink too much alcohol (these two things often coincide). When I'm feeling sympathetic to my body's intent, I see it as a warped way of my body-mind trying to protect itself. If I've been triggered or I'm too stressed about something, my brain decides the best thing to do is to shut itself down for the day; to put a do-not-disturb sign on my life. It seems, questionably, to work. I have to call in sick to work, I have to cancel my plans with friends – there's no way I can sit upright, let alone run a workshop or have a coffee with an acquaintance. With migraines or any chronic illness, your sense of time and priority becomes warped. All you can focus on is the present, the excruciating pain in your head. You can't think of tomorrow or two years ago – it makes it so that you can only focus on the here and now. It's indeed a strange way of introducing mindfulness to your routine.

As well as its impacts on health, sexual violence can, perhaps unsurprisingly, have a direct impact on your sex life. From pregnancies to sexually transmitted diseases, the physical after-effects can be grave. Physical effects on our sex organs can also persist years after sexual violence. Prior sexual assault is considered a risk factor for conditions like vaginismus, in which pelvic muscles spasm upon sexual penetration, causing pain and inability to have sex. It's also considered a risk factor for vulvodynia. I was fifteen when my vulva started hurting. I had a long-term boyfriend, and we were having timid, teenage sex. After we'd finished (or more, *he'd* finished, as was the norm for heterosexual teenage sex in 2011), a burn began spreading across my vulva. It ripped through me, indiscriminately, making my whole vulval area feel like it was on fire, being ripped open and grated at the same time. I cried (the poor boy didn't know what to do) and shouted for ice to cool down the fire. What was wrong with me? Was this normal? Was I allergic to cum? Was I allergic to sex?

This demon of pain returned intermittently in the years following this first incident. I'd have a one-night stand and have to grit my teeth in the aftermath, waiting for the body next to me to go to sleep before I could sneak out to douse my vulva in cold water and wet tissues. I stopped being able to insert tampons at age seventeen, when it became too painful and uncomfortable. Even pads aggravated the area, yet I tried to persist (this was before the boom of period pants, which now are my saving grace).

For a few years, in my early twenties, the pain lay dormant, and I was having sex mostly pain-free for a while. I had flings, then I fell in love with my current partner and our sex life was great. Then, about a year ago, the fire came back. I can have sex painlessly and indeed pleasurably, but afterwards, the pain begins to burn, radiating around my vulva area. I googled:

> burning pain after sex / stinging vagina / vagina feels like it's on fire after sex.

My questions were immediately answered: I have vulvo-dynia. Specifically, the provoked, intermittent type affecting my whole vulva. I also have frequent bouts of bacterial vaginosis, vulval eczema and thrush. Basically, my vulva is frequently pissed off. For those who haven't heard the term before, vulvodynia literally means vulva (vulvo) pain (dynia). Pain in the vulva. That's your vagina, clit, labia, perineum – basically anything that's 'down there'. Apart from the knowledge that there's a problem with the nerves in the vulva and the pelvic floor, it's relatively unknown what causes it or why it happens – like so many other feminised illnesses – but there are a couple of theories. For me, the theory of causation most appropriate is that which links the condition to previous sexual trauma.

Doctors believe sexual trauma can cause vulvodynia in two ways: nerve damage from the actual incident of violence, or nerve damage from the ongoing tension survivors brace themselves against (often subconsciously) whilst having consensual sex. My experience mostly falls into the latter of the two. Despite my years of aching (quite literally) to be liberated and sex-positive, I had a difficult and complicated relationship with sex and sexual partners. I became fearful of sex, and this fear contributed to a vicious cycle: I'd be afraid of sex but would still want to have it with my partner and the fear would make me tense and tight, leading to further pain during and after penetrative sex – I would be afraid of sex (rinse and repeat). My body tried to warn me, and I'd ignore it, insisting to myself that I was *fine*. Once again, it rings true: the body always keeps the score – and that score is often traumatically painful. I've never been to the doctor about this - I'm one of millions of people with vulvas who haven't. Instead, I'm still in the process of learning to cope alone, with the ears of my lover, my therapist and my friends to help me through.

I've worked out what helps and what doesn't. What helps: cotton underwear (lace is overrated), cold showers after sex (very cosy and romantic), no tight trousers, cutting holes in tights when I'm having a flare-up. The common tips with sex are to take things slowly, to use lots of lube and ensure you're aroused with lots of foreplay before penetration. I would add to this list the key treatments of patience and masturbation. There is no quick fix to this sort of pain. I learned that talking about it helps, especially with your partner. We communicated and he came to understand the difficult feelings I have around my pain and its effect on my libido. I also try to masturbate more. Partnered sex can be scary when it becomes a really painful experience, so exploring sex with yourself can be a safe way to ease back into sexuality. It might take weeks, months, even years, but if I've enjoyed sex previously, I know I'll be able to enjoy it again. I'm hopeful that there is a way back to painless, and more importantly joyful, sex.

The trauma I've experienced and the physical symptoms I live with are indubitably connected. If my body has been in a stress response every day for the past two decades, then it's inevitable that, as a result, I'm going to be tense; in pain, I'll struggle with sleep and I'll feel fatigued. My trauma became trapped in my body at a young age, and it still doesn't know how to get out. It might be sewn into my whole body by now, creeping through my muscles, my nerves and my brain whenever it pleases. If my body learned to repress violence at a young age, place it deep in the body, how would it have known any differently when it came to the later violations?

I still believe that my musculoskeletal pain, despite now being shown to have a physical cause, is strongly linked with my survival. Even more, I know that my migraines and my vulvodynia are a direct result of the stress and trauma I've persisted through. So perhaps conversion disorder does indeed exist, perhaps there has been a somatisation of the trauma – that doesn't mean it has to be diminished. Pain caused by trauma is still pain, and ranking types of pain is of help to no one. The problem is more with the ways in which the medical industry perceives psychogenic illnesses, not with the mere fact that they might exist. Even if conditions have a psychological, trauma-based root, the research is still needed, care is always still needed. The medical system needs to be holistically trauma-focused. Instead of dismissing pain rooted in trauma, we need to look at the whole body-mind existence. It is not a dead end to see trauma as a cause of pain; instead, it should be a beginning.

# Chapter 8

# The Ways We Cope

**Trigger warnings: drug and alcohol abuse, self-harm, disordered eating and vomiting**

When we experience assault or abuse, the ensuing feelings and memories can be incredibly painful. To numb what feels like an unbearable amount of pain, we often employ a plethora of coping mechanisms. Our feelings can be so overwhelming that it feels like the only way we can deal with them is to avoid them altogether. There have been many times when I know I'm in deep emotional pain; I know there's something I need to address within myself but doing so is just too hard. As outlined in the previous chapter, when a person has higher ACEs, there's a higher likelihood of engaging in risky coping behaviours. These coping behaviours include ones we stereotypically expect to see – drinking, smoking and taking drugs. They also include ones we don't think of so much, like self-harm and eating disorders.

Statistics on the relationship between surviving sexual violence and developing problems with using substances as a coping mechanism vary. One study found that out of a group of people who were seeking treatment for alcohol use disorder, 49 per cent of the women involved and 12 per cent of the men reported experiencing childhood sexual abuse. The experience of sexual abuse is also thought to more deeply entrench someone's dependency on alcohol, with survivors of childhood sexual abuse being 25 per cent more likely to relapse into addiction and to do so within half the time frame as non-survivors. In terms of survivors of sexual violence in adulthood, women who were survivors of rape were 13.4 times more likely than non-survivors to develop a problem with alcohol and 26 times more likely to develop a problem with drugs.

Upon writing this chapter, I realised that I myself am a frightful muddle of many of these risky coping mechanisms. A couple of years ago, whilst I was simultaneously dealing with fallout from my childhood abuse along with the process of reporting sexual assault to the Metropolitan Police, the only way I could get through some nights was by drinking a bottle of red wine, alone. I had a loving partner, an amazing flatmate and the best friends I could wish for, but all I wanted to do was sit alone in my bed drinking wine, listening to the saddest album I knew, fully immersed in my pain. I was in a major depressive episode, and the only thing that made me feel anything that wasn't pure dread and despair was that bottle of wine every night. Thirty to forty per cent of survivors experience depression and almost one-third (31 per cent) have experienced PTSD after surviving sexual violence, and in the throes of these conditions, drinking or being intoxicated can help us in a few ways. They can numb us so we don't feel the pain as intensely, they can distract us so that we can keep ourselves in denial, and they can help us to release some of the pain that has become trapped within us. I've drunk myself to oblivion and almost overdosed for all three of these reasons.

There's also another end of the spectrum when it comes to why I have turned to alcohol and drugs in the past. Hyperactivity and recklessness are often seen in symptoms of post-traumatic stress, especially in c-PTSD. When I am in a hypomanic episode, I feel like I'm on fire inside and substances act as one of two solutions in this situation. They will either keep that fire going, stoking it so I don't become extinguished, a fate equal to death in my psyche during those times, or else they will send me spiralling into a pit of helpless despair. My mind is racing; my insides feel like they're exploding. The only way I can attempt to dull it down is to drink six beers, a bottle of wine, or five vodka mixers. It's the only way I can try to keep myself afloat in the burning despair of the final stages of my hypomania.

Some of my coping mechanisms come hand in hand. One drink turns into another, which then turns into accepting a bump of coke, which then turns to organising more coke for whoever is around me, which then turns to going wild and staying up for hours in a pub or a random person's house, which then turns to sleeping with a stranger who gives me fleeting validation for a few hours. I wish I knew how to counteract these patterns when they emerge, but when the wanting takes hold, it becomes near-impossible to resist. Our ways of coping can overtake us, possess us even, and these incidents can be life-ruining for many.

★

Since being a teenager, I have fantasised about, and sometimes acted upon, harming myself. A typical behaviour for
someone who's been through a lot of trauma, self-harm
can act as a way of controlling the pain and turmoil we
feel internally. Up to 79 per cent of those who self-harm
report experiencing sexual and/or physical abuse in their
childhood. Another study found that female survivors of
CSA were four times more likely to have an incident of
self-harm. When we think of self-harm, we may explicitly refer to cutting or burning oneself. I have previously
consciously harmed myself, cutting myself and hitting myself
in my deepest panics and despairs. Yet I also subconsciously
harm myself, exhibiting dermatophagia, a disorder where
one bites at or picks their skin. I also have elements of
trichollotomania, twisting and pulling strands of my hair
out. The latter can occur both as a lazy, self-soothing habit,
or when I'm extremely stressed. The nail/skin biting and
picking is a bad habit that I mindlessly engage in, just like
anyone who bites their nails, but it also acts as a painful
way of self-soothing when I'm stressed or emotionally overwhelmed. The biting, the pain, brings me back to myself.
It allows me to ground myself and focus on the present,
even if in the most uncomfortable way possible. It's like a
nervous tick, my instant ointment when I'm stressed to any
degree. I've been trying to condition myself to stop, wearing
plasters over my fingers or trying to pay keen attention to
when I'm biting; but when I am overwhelmed, if I have
an argument with my partner, a friend is upset with me
or I can't sleep, I bite my thumbnail skin to a damaging
extent, drawing blood and risking infection. I do it now
as I write these words, having to apply the medical tape

I keep by the side of my writing desk for use during the writing of a triggering chapter.

Even if I don't often act on conscious self-harming impulses, I still often fantasise or obsess over them, especially when my mental health begins to deteriorate, and my trauma response is triggered. Everyone experiences intrusive thoughts, but those who struggle with depression and anxiety disorders often see those intrusive thoughts become darker and more graphic as other parts of their mind begin to slip into more unstable places.

In popular society we are told that people with eating disorders must fit their typical boxes: a pretty, already slim girl who wants to be a model and stops eating completely, exercising excessively, or a woman who binges food and purges it out every night because she has body dysmorphia and is depressed about her weight. I thought I wasn't entitled to call what I had an eating disorder because my primary motivation for it wasn't body dysmorphia and wanting to lose weight. What's often overlooked is the numerous different ways that eating disorders can manifest, and the ways that we all deserve help if we're struggling with patterns of disordered eating. I don't know what label I have or had; somewhere on the cusp of anorexia, bulimia or in the elusive EDNOS (eating disorder not otherwise specified) category. It's not solely about food intake, not solely about purging. That liminal space becomes apparent again, as with so much else in the aftermath of trauma.

After talking it through in therapy, it turns out that my attitude to food and controlling it stems from multiple complex sources (there's that word 'complex', again). The firmest root was wanting to be in control of myself and my body. Having my body taken from me so many times and losing my own mind so often, I thought I'd found a trick by strictly monitoring my food intake and expelling it if I was unhappy about it. I finally felt secure and in control. I'm not alone in this attempt of a solution – it's been found that around 30 per cent of patients being treated for eating disorders had been abused in childhood. Moreover, those who've experienced childhood sexual abuse as well as rape in adulthood were found to have extremely high levels of disordered eating. The correlation is even higher when focusing on specific disorders such as bulimia nervosa and binge-eating disorder.

Yet, almost instantly after discovering my new 'trick', I desperately started spinning out of control. It wasn't a matter of my choice but an obsession with the food I ate and a compulsion to throw up after eating. My days revolved around food. The few times I ate, I felt intolerable shame and would purge it out. The eating disorder became ritualistic: monitor what I eat, purge it all out, feel 'better' (momentarily). I was so weak and tired, constantly planning the next few calories I could convince myself to eat. Each day I would write what I could manage and spend the rest of my time thinking about food and hunger, with my brain fog caused by malnutrition obscuring most of these thoughts anyway. I kept up appearances, going for dinner with friends and throwing up in the toilets after eating. I lost a lot of weight and my skin became translucent. People told me I looked amazing, looked *so healthy*. They couldn't fathom that this was reinforcing the harm I was doing to myself as a good thing, was telling me that being unhealthily thin would earn me praise.

Although I say it wasn't about losing weight, losing it and becoming dangerously thin became a by-product of my initial urge. I associated thinness with this taking back of control, and the praise I received from well-intended outsiders intensified the aim of skinniness. As well as the praise from outside, praise came internally too. When I hit that desired weight on the scales, when I could see a thigh gap widening, when I could see my clavicle sticking out, it was working. I was in control after all. The ritual of the eating disorder was expanded: monitor what you eat, purge it all out, feel 'better', become thinner, gain praise, and repeat. In a fatphobic world, my thinness had always been praised. From a young age, I was referred to as 'tiny', 'skinny', 'petite'. To become anything other than that felt like a loss of some, albeit arbitrary, identity that had been reinforced in me throughout my whole life.

The vomiting worked as a way of both maintaining the calorie intake and purging myself as a coping mechanism. I'd purge to rid myself of 'bad' foods, or any food I'd consumed at all. I'd also purge when I was overwhelmed with anxiety or fear, or if the urge to do so simply happened to pop in my head as a compulsion that couldn't be resisted. One therapist associated it with a tendency for OCD, the obsessive thoughts being to empty myself and maintain hollowness and the compulsion being to vomit as soon as the idea came into my mind. As with many other survivors of abuse, specifically childhood sexual abuse, the act of purging or vomiting works to cleanse the shame and anxiety out of my insides. We feel dirty for the abuse that occurred to us and society's subsequent shaming that makes us feel like the problem is within *us* and not the perpetrator. The stickiness of shame is hard to get out. So, the best option seems to be to throw it up, exorcise it from ourselves. The shame always returns, but those few moments of peace after purging make everything feel briefly OK. When we vomit, our body releases endorphins that make us feel good. I became addicted to this enforced natural high. For those who've never engaged in such behaviours or been drawn to them, this might seem confusing and disgusting. But there's a twisted sense of achievement and self-preservation in these acts of coping.

Around my third 'episode', I decided to seek help from the doctors. I went to my GP and told them I'd been struggling with disordered eating. I was down to 800 calories a day, I was vomiting after every meal and obsessing over these rituals constantly. My GP weighed me and booked me in for an ECG and blood test to check I wasn't doing any 'serious' physical damage to myself. After they'd been carried out, I could apparently pursue pathways to therapy to discover the roots of my eating disorder. I was pretty sure I already knew the roots, but accessing professional help for my eating disorders was something I really needed. I needed someone to help me fully grasp why I was making my body deteriorate and how I could find a path to some recovery to protect myself.

When the results of the blood tests came back, everything they had tested came back as 'normal'. In a similar fashion to my other illnesses, it was a seemingly positive outcome. However, as a sick person trying to seek help, it was another result that meant my problems weren't taken seriously. Next was the ECG – an electrocardiogram – that tested how my heart was being affected by my self-enforced malnourishment. I can still see this ECG now; its beautiful red lines showing the steady rise and fall of my still-healthy heart. The results came back as 'normal' again. I felt embarrassed. I wasn't doing any serious damage to my body, so why was I making such a big deal about this?

I went back to my GP and they once again confirmed nothing atypical had shown up on my tests. Did I still want help? I could come back and be weighed again in a few weeks' time and they could see if I could be referred to the eating disorders unit. I agreed, but subsequently failed to organise the next appointment. I resigned myself to dealing with it on my own. I already carried so much shame around the eating disorder and how it could so easily come to rule my life at any given time. It felt too much to expose myself to the doctors and specialists who would judge me solely on my BMI and ignore me if I wasn't thin enough. They implied that I would only be allowed help if I hit a certain low weight, and although I was well below the recommended BMI (an already problematic scale) for my height, it wasn't enough. Would I need to force myself to drop to an even lower weight to deserve help? Another form of impostor syndrome reared its ugly head: I wasn't ill enough, didn't have a real eating disorder, so why was I trying to take a place in these already over-demanded services? I felt let down by the support in place even before I was allowed access to it. I decided to wait for it to wash over me, to wait for some unplaceable shift to occur as it had in the episodes before to return me to my fleeting normality. The return to normalcy came, and then I reverted back again. Then I recovered again, then I relapsed again.

The thought patterns still come back every so often, like a bad friend you thought you'd left behind. Feeling out of control triggers it. Feeling abandoned, another form of losing control, triggers it to the extreme. I became comforted by the fact I can always turn to it when I feel I'm losing myself. It felt like my special secret, the one piece of armour that I'll always have. I told myself that it was fine if I was abandoned, because I had myself, and having myself meant monitoring myself, punishing myself to show me how much I cared. A twisted logic, like an abusive relationship with myself, but one that stuck with me for a long time. I still don't know how to talk about it out loud. This section flowed out of me in writing, but the words become too difficult to speak aloud to friends and family. I worry that if I ever mention it when it's returning, my patterns will be constantly monitored, my coping mechanism ripped away from me, leaving me untethered. I've talked to some loved ones about it in hushed tones, never fully revealing the intricacies of the compulsions. It is a deeply secret coping mechanism, and the one I try hardest to leave behind each time.

★

One key reason I've been able to cope in the aftermath of sexual violence – and a vital part in my having the capacity to write this very book – is therapy. Therapy of all forms: talking therapies with a trained counsellor, group therapies, writing, talking to loved ones, resting.

In 2017, after the fourteen-month wait for talking therapy, I got to the top of the list. This therapist was in a doctor's-surgery attic room. This therapist and I connected, and then we abruptly didn't. The first few sessions went well, I told her about my childhood sexual abuse, and I cried in front of her – something I rarely do with anyone, let alone a therapist I'd only met twice. Then, I was sexually assaulted. The session after the assault had occurred, I confided in her everything that had happened just a few days before. I can't remember specifically what she said, or what her reaction was, but it wasn't what I needed. She didn't refer me to Rape Crisis, didn't tell me to attend The Havens, the sexual-assault referral centre a mere twenty-minute walk away. She didn't talk me through any of my options, and instead forced me to turn inwards to deal with my trauma immediately. I wasn't ready for this. She got me to access anger and pain I wasn't yet ready to feel. I wasn't at first cognisant of the fact that she'd let me down, but after the events unfolded, I closed up. I stopped telling her my real feelings, and ultimately, I stopped going, missing the last two appointments as I went home to stay with my parents to physically recover from the assault. Perhaps she hadn't been trained in what to do if a patient discloses current abuse occurring, though that would surprise me greatly. Perhaps she did refer me to the services, and I have blocked it out of my mind. The time is hazy, and I look back at it through clouded glass. Perhaps I projected my anger and disdain towards her, when it was really about the man who had taken my body from me. Perhaps there was nothing she could have really done for me in those moments − I'll never know.

After that disappointment, I wanted to avoid therapy for a while. However, a few months later, when I did ultimately attend The Havens, I jumped at the offer of one-to-one counselling. The waiting list was only two weeks. Fourteen months down to two weeks? It seemed I'd struck gold − all I'd had to do was be sexually assaulted! My therapist was a kind Eastern European woman, who I'll call Margaret, who clearly cared about her patients a lot. However, we never fully connected. Maybe that had something to do with the fact I was ordered to not talk about the actual rape in rape counselling because anything I said could be used against me in court. At the time, this was standard practice across all counselling services for survivors of sexual violence, and following campaigns to remove this protocol, The Havens and other services have subsequently changed this. It's not that I didn't trust Margaret herself, but that I was directly told not to trust the space, that anything I said could and would be held against me, and she could facilitate that, however indirectly. Again, the following memories are through frosted glass. To a large degree, I ignored the official advice given to refrain from talking about the rape. I talked openly about the assault, about the previous assaults I'd suffered and the childhood sexual abuse I'd survived. Perhaps a part of me knew my case wouldn't make it to court, so I saw the opportunity to use the therapy for what I actually needed, without the fear of my deepest words being used against me.

After a few sessions with her, she told me that a new spot had opened up on the group therapy sessions. I'd always wanted to attend group therapy. Having previously found it hard to discuss living with trauma with people who didn't, in my opinion, *get it*, I had so wanted to find those who did. I wanted to find a group who would know what I was thinking without me having to speak it, who would know of the endless nights and hopeless moments when reality crumbles away. This fantasy wasn't exactly what I found. We were eight women thrown into an impersonal room to try and navigate our trauma together. Things could have been different, but I found myself closed up again after the first session. In that first session, the heaviness of surviving multiple abuses – in childhood and adulthood – gripped my body. I sobbed and sobbed, my usual defence mechanisms failing me. No boundaries had been established as to whether we were allowed to touch one another, hug one another, comfort one another, so no one did. We were shoved into this room with two facilitators, and I felt unanchored. I felt like I was in a foreign country with a group of strangers who couldn't understand the language I was sobbing in.

Ultimately, I think someone did comfort me. One of the facilitators likely intervened, asked if I needed anything and gave me a tissue. But those moments did damage I never came back from. The time between being unanchored and being found could have been seconds or hours. My body-mind had learned that vulnerability wouldn't bring me comfort, only pain. So, I closed up. I physically returned to every session but was never fully in the room again. I performed the role of the good survivor, said what people wanted to hear, gave the advice I knew I should be giving, yet I was detached, at arm's length from the other women and the room.

I went another year without therapy, and then chose to have some private, affordable online therapy. I shouldn't have had to pay for private therapy, but my desperation led me to realms outside the failing NHS. This therapist was fine, nothing extraordinary. I opened up, and then again, I closed up. The trend continued. She said something I disagreed with, and instead of discussing this with her, I decided to alienate her instead. Around the same time, I was beginning to record my podcast with the BBC. Part of the contract with the BBC was that we had an on-call therapist for the series who would be available as and when we needed her, and who would talk to guests beforehand to check they were in a safe enough place mentally to take part in the series.

My producers told me that the higher-ups had demanded I would need to be screened by this therapist before we began recording the series. My trust issues set in – were they testing me? Trying to determine whether I was too crazy to be recording a series for them? My producers tried to assure me that the purpose of the call was to establish a rapport with the therapist and to give me the support I needed. I felt like it was a trap, that if I said the wrong thing, the whole series would be cancelled. I had to perform, maintain my sanity to show that I was a good enough survivor to host this series. The therapist herself was nice enough, but my disdain for the purpose of the session overpowered my outlook.

After all those years, my greatest therapist love was a secondary-care psychotherapist with the NHS. In 2019, my mental health deteriorated again. I was suicidal and erratic; I knew I needed help. NHS talking therapies were out of the question – I needed the big guns. I was referred for secondary-care treatment, attending outpatient appointments for assessments at Lewisham Hospital's secure patient unit. The psychiatrists there were kind and referred me to a psychologist and a psycho-therapist. This was when I was officially diagnosed with c-PTSD with a tendency for emotional instability (again, a terribly feminised diagnosis). The therapist I worked with, let's call her Fiona, was wonderful – she was the first therapist I've ever felt truly 'got me'. She helped me, literally, draw everything out on paper and denote the vicious cycles that present in my mind when things become overwhelming. She let me sit and be silent, let me talk endlessly; she let me be myself.

This wonderful therapist sadly moved departments, so our sessions were cut short. I was supposed to see her for six months, but this was shortened to just two months. Once again, I was placed back on the waiting list. The coronavirus pandemic has meant this waiting list has been frozen. It's been over a year since I've heard from them. My mental illnesses have been relatively stable during this time (surprisingly, lockdown fitted me to a tee), but I fear for when the next episode may strike. I also fear for all those on the list so deeply in need, alone and overwhelmed by the realities of mental illness.

I have the privilege of having a new private therapist now. She's no Fiona, but it's still early days. It'll take me a while to get over Fiona. It seems to be going well. Like dating, we have to take it slow, get to know each other. If it doesn't work out, that's OK, I'll go on the counselling directory once more, like returning to a dating app in the aftermath of a failed fling. Therapy is hard. It's not fun, but it's the realest sense of the often-overused phrase, 'self-care'. It is a dredging up, a constant processing, a brain-drain of an activity to take part in every week. It's not always perfect, but it works, grounding me and carving out a space for me to vent about my internal world for an hour every week.

Some of the most visceral words I've ever read came from Pam Allyn: 'Reading is breathing in; writing is breathing out.' Reading blog posts, Tumblr and Reddit pages about the world, mental health and trauma saved me as a teenager. Living with such heavy secrets, I felt seen in anonymous spaces where people had the same secrets. As I grew older, books on philosophy and sociology, feminist and cultural critiques, helped me understand the confusing world around me. Writing has always felt like an explosion on a page, or equally like being dragged by my fingertips, searching in the dark to find anything to steady myself. I can become enchanted, engrossed – nothing else mattering.

My longest episode of mania came in the form of poems and prose. I couldn't sleep, couldn't think of anything but the page and the ink, the interconnectedness, the blurring of me and my words. I didn't sleep, for the electricity in my mind made it so that I couldn't do anything but write, fingers to black keys or dusty biros to crumpled paper. I forget about writing sometimes, forget the release it gives me. The opening of a faucet that sputters and groans with the feelings that pour from my throat. I go into a trance, forget my surroundings, hearing my voice in my mind: erratic or calm, collected or anxious, crazy or all of these things at once. The trance is blurry and fixating, it makes me forget where I am. I have been like this for many years, pouring myself onto the page even when I can't stand up straight or my mind betrays me. It is a haven I cocoon myself in. I can translate my mind's messiness in some comprehensible vomit, confusing and beautiful all at once.

It is both therapy and the pain itself. A codependent relationship. It bleeds me dry and replenishes me. I remember going into these writing trances throughout my life, in my childhood bedroom or in the classroom. Head to page as I blur my eyes and let my hands do the talking. My hand is plugged into my mind (I guess it quite literally is), the nerves and veins taking over and guiding my thoughts onto the page. Maybe it was about friendship or wanting to throw myself away (out of the window). I birth the words, phrases and feelings I need to see to continue.

Whilst trying to remind people that they are more than just their trauma and more than the things done to their bodies, I have, ironically, made my life's work up to now about my trauma. I guess it's the old adage, 'Do as I say, not as I do.' Could it be a form of workaholism, converting my inner turmoils into the work I do every day? Is it another way for me to stay in control? If I can spend all my energy on reading and writing about trauma, maybe I don't have to truly confront the pain within me. If I can intellectualise the pain, maybe that will finally help me understand these awful things that I was subjected to? Is it also a way to show the world that I'm worthy, that I'm the 'good survivor' who can talk about their trauma with beautiful words and inspire others to keep going? Back to complexity, once again – maybe it's my lifeline in numerous ways: a healthy outlet and a way of distracting myself, a way of proving myself as worthy and avoiding the real pain, and a therapeutic passion that helps me make sense of the mess.

Another form of therapy for me has always been rest and sleep. Sleep has long been the love of my life. I wrote my master's dissertation on the concept of rest as a resistive act, primarily because it's the thing I spend most of my time doing. I sleep a lot. People think I work a ton, and I guess I do – but most of it is done from bed, or at least with copious amounts of napping time between writing. I sleep through the night and I usually take a nap in the middle of the day. I lie down in bed and write, I lie down in bed and talk to my loved ones, I lie down in bed when I'm feeling unwell and when I'm feeling better. I've equally had my share of not being able to sleep, staying up until 3 a.m. because my mind won't stop whirring, either with worries and memories or new ideas.

These nights slow down as I watch the clock, aching for sleep to come. Like Alison Kafer's concept of 'crip time' ('crip' being the reclaimed term used by disabled communities), and Taraneh Fazeli's 'sleepy time' (both concepts which I ascribe to), I follow a 'survivor time'. The two prior concepts denote the different conception of time that disabled and chronically ill people live with. As a disabled person, I live in crip time: days of no work, days of working erratically, not turning up to the event, sleeping for twelve hours, not being able to find the words I want at the speech I'm giving. This is inherently linked to my survival and the trauma that has caused my disabilities. Survivor time has its own defining features: needing to go slower with sex, taking your time to process the trauma you're experiencing, remembering a decade after the abuse occurred. It's a way of experiencing the world and our space in it, a way of slowing down and allowing our traumatised selves compassion in how we live. We may need to sleep more, we may need to process alone or with other people, we may take longer to complete tasks because it's too hard to go outside in a traumatised state. If we change our concept of time, we can try to learn that we're not abnormal if we can't adhere to the fastness of modern life.

# 4

# Relationships

# Chapter 9

# All I Know of Sex

The contemporary question of 'body counts' (how many people you've had sex with) is often a paradoxical one: on either side of the spectrum, you're afraid that your number is too large or too small. In typical binary fashion, they tend to say that men overexaggerate their number (for kudos) and women underexaggerate (for fear of being seen as a slut). If someone were to ask my own 'body count', and I knew them well enough, I would happily tell them my number (I will not be telling you the number, but, hint: I'm proud of being a slut). What I often don't add, however, is the trauma laced through the number of men I have slept with in that count.

All of the times with the men I do 'count' were consensual, but many of them were unhealthy encounters. There were many nights of me trying to force my body into a healing that would not come. Nights spent pretending that I was OK, drinking too much alcohol and taking too many drugs, then craving the warmth of someone's skin to help me through the comedown. Nights, days, months of craving love so much that I would allow anyone access to my body. I'd allow entry to anyone and everyone who I thought could make me feel whole, if only for a few moments. Yet it never made me feel whole. One-night stands of dangerous, drunken, intoxicated and unprotected sex would fill a temporary hole that left me empty and aching in the aftermath.

I wanted to be a 'normal' person in my twenties: liberated, up for anything. But I wasn't 'normal', and regardless, normality is a myth. I didn't let myself grieve for my body and the trauma it had endured. I myself was the pushy friend making me go out, the person making me have sex when I didn't really want to. I was the one who pushed my own boundaries, a toxic re-enactment of the past abuses I'd experienced. I needed to try to fix the past by re-enacting it, showing myself that there was an alternative ending to the times I had been harmed. This was a state of hypersexuality – a trait common with survivors of sexual violence. I wanted to be in control, wanted to be desired. I didn't want to be seen as broken – I needed to prove to these random men (and ultimately, to myself) that I could still enjoy sex. I needed to show the fuckboys I dated that I was OK, that I wasn't too damaged, that I could still be fucked. Although responsibility should be placed on harm-doers, I often also ended up placing myself in potentially harmful situations. I'm not blaming myself, but rather accentuating the fact that our past trauma can place us in further future dangers. I didn't understand consent or mutual respect; didn't understand the ways I could try to rediscover and recover myself in a safe and controlled way, as opposed to a dangerously controlling way.

The word 'consent' still scares me. It's like a thicket I can't see through, and I'm scared of things I can't see through, of things I don't understand. If I'm writing a book about the lived experience of sexual violence then surely I must have an opinion on consent? The truth is, I don't know how I feel about the concept of consent. Thinking about it sends my body into overdrive. All of the unnamed 'things' I've alluded to throughout this book start to swarm my body. The incidents found in the infinite grey make the thicket even harder to see through. Looking back, when it came to what I'd perceived as consensual sex, oftentimes I hadn't really wanted to have sex. But I usually thought that, as I'd gotten myself into that situation, it was too late to say no. Who was I to reject this man now, after I'd invited him back, or been the person to hit on him in the first place? *It'd be too awkward to stop – I may as well just get it over and done with.* I'd force myself to consent to avoid any hassle.

Women are largely still socialised to appease, socialised to please the men we sleep with (I speak only of these matters in reference to heterosexual relations, as they're the only ones I've experienced this deep discomfort with). We're told that consent is simple: wherever we go, yes means yes and no means no. To confirm, I do believe that no does assuredly mean no. But does yes always mean yes? All the times included in my 'count' were consensual, but many of them were still 'off' in some unplaceable way. These are the instances that often make my stomach turn, my skin crawl. I hear rape culture taunt me in my head: *you just regret having sex with them.* But it wasn't just bad sex (I've had plenty of that). Really, I don't regret having sex with them. Instead, I regret (or more aptly, grieve for) the circumstances and environment in which those sexual encounters came about.

The trouble with these times wasn't even really the individual scenarios or men themselves, but the societal conditioning that surrounded our two bodies. I would put pressure on myself, for I had been socialised to please, socialised to find it easier to get it over and done with. The men would be socialised to seek pleasure first, to touch before asking. I would usually be seeking validation or a way to rewrite the endings of my own traumatic past. These unplaceable times would often find our gendered selves falling into our written roles. Was it the drink leading us to lazily fit our stereotypes, or perhaps the inherent pressure of modern intimacy? The man would be dominant, in charge, focused on his orgasm. I would be going through the motions, perhaps in pain, likely numb. Neither of us would talk about it and would roll over and fall asleep when he came. To be clear, I'm not saying every sexual encounter I've had whilst drunk played out in this way. The first night I slept with my current partner, we were both very drunk, silly and spontaneous. But on that night, I started panicking midway through having sex. Instead of forcing myself to grin and bear it or being abandoned mid-panic attack, which has happened on numerous occasions, we stopped, he held me, and we listened to calming music from a TV show we'd both just finished. There was mutual respect and care. Even if we were drunk, there was a level of communication that was constantly maintained – a level that wasn't there in the unplaceable times.

This brings us to the crux of what I think (or *think* I think; I still can't see too clearly) consent means. Consent means communication. Or more than that, consent is inseparable from communication. Communication about what you both want, communication about how you're feeling and what you need, communication that you can stop having sex whenever you want. It needs to become normal to have conversations about sex, to see verbalising consent as a healthy, normal part of a sexual encounter, rather than an awkward formality. It should be a cultural norm for any partner to ask the other what feels good, what they need to feel pleasure. Communication is both verbal and non-verbal. Although verbal cues are always important, and need to become the go-to, non-verbal cues are equally important. We must pay attention to the way we move, the way we moan, the pace we each need to go at.

This act of paying attention to non-verbal cues seems to be one based in the skill of empathy – a skill previously discussed as being difficult at times for some that conform to society's tropes of masculinity to access. Can empathy, deep understanding and connection be 'taught' in a conventional sense in our current sex-education classes? Can we teach boys to value their partner's pleasure on an equal par to their own with our current systems? Or, more likely, is a radical change needed throughout all of our socialisations and educations? As opposed to the toxic masculinity and male entitlement currently ingrained in our boys and young men, what should instead be ingrained is the attentiveness and reciprocity found in a more tender masculinity. Masculinity itself does not have to be a bad thing — we should not want to do away with it completely, for masculinity can come in an endless array of shapes and sizes. Perhaps a more general shift towards this tender masculinity would have the desired knock-on effect of nourishing empathy and care in the men of our future.

Most men nowadays won't think of themselves as misogynists. They will assume they understand consent and will believe that they would never harm a partner. To accusations of sexual violence, the average man might retort that what happened was consensual, that the accuser's account is simply wrong — and they may very well believe that claim. What we need to be asking is what these men believe consent to mean.

The common route of denial and shame in responding to accusations of sexual violence speaks to the way many abusers won't even realise what they've done is harmful. Although the world shames men into denying all wrongdoing to avoid accountability and maintain their coveted innocence, many of them are also wilfully ignorant. I'm not speaking here of more purposeful, calculatedly abusive acts of harm. I am instead talking of the 'blurred lines' so often alluded to. The male harm-doers may indeed remember the moments in question as consensual because they've been indoctrinated to misunderstand what consent actually is. They may — very wrongly — believe a coerced 'yes' is consent, or silence is consent, or that blackout drunk sex is consensual. Again, this all comes back to the education surrounding consent and active communication. If men felt empowered to talk about sex with their partner, especially before any sexual relationship has occurred, many harmful situations could perhaps be avoided. Many men see talking about sex as embarrassing, awkward or feminine. To avoid our boys becoming men who harm women, we need to encourage them to talk openly about sex and their feelings towards it. We need to encourage them to want to talk about sex with women, to see it as a part of the process of love and relationships, instead of leaving communication as solely the burden of the feminine partner to take on. Consent doesn't have to necessarily be sexy, but it should have to be talked about in an open and understanding way.

Plenty of times throughout my young life, I've been told, or it has been inferred, that I am 'too much' plenty of times throughout my life. When I was sixteen, on drugs and frequently breaking down at parties, mean girls told me I was 'weird' and 'crazy'. Numerous fuckboys have ghosted me after I've had a panic attack. I was told I was unstable, clingy, crazy. Even if these terms were only explicitly said to me a handful of times, the ghosting and aversion to me once we'd had sex told me loud and clear that my traumatised, loud and proud self was too much for them. I'm startlingly translucent in my romantic endeavours. I tell people how I feel; when I'm falling in love with them or when I feel like I want to die. They either take it or leave it, but when they leave it, I can't deny that I feel crushed. I wish I could say *fuck them,* could laugh about it with my friends afterwards and actually mean it, but I'm still insecure, scrambling at the rocks of validation and security. Kelsey Lu, one of my favourite musicians, has a song called 'Too Much'.

When I saw her perform this song live, she pre-empted the song saying that it was for all the people who were worried they'd been 'too much', that they're too 'crazy', 'needy', 'hysterical'. Lu's answer to our worries: you are all of these things and more, and that's beautiful.

I am traumatised, ill, in pain, scared, lonely, loving, open and honest – but not too much. Lu sings, *is my heart too much for you?* The answer is that they're not enough for *us*, emptying themselves to be the vessels of masculinity they believe they need to be. I want to ascribe to a feminine, queer, crip form of love, rather than the empty sort of vessel. Love that is tender, gentle, open and giving. Where we can cry on the phone, have a breakdown in the bar, repeatedly text, repeatedly call, say I love you, and that be more than enough – never too much.

I have always craved love, been desperate for it. I craved requited adoration from the mean pretty-boys I used to chase. Yet, before embracing my too-muchness with open arms, I kept this craving quiet. I pretended I was chill, cool, happy with the casual sex they would give me in rations. I needed to seem normal, to be the liberated sex-positive feminist pronounced as our common goal. I forced myself to seem detached, to play the cool girl I thought was a prerequisite for being a modern girl–woman. But I've never liked casual sex. I really despise emotionless sex. I can only orgasm or truly enjoy sex when I feel strong emotions and true intimacy with the person I am having sex with. Where had this smothering message I'd heard come from, that to be liberated we must be having constant, unadulterated, unattached sex? Why has this modern ideal for sex become such a masculinist one: detached, rational, objective? What about the feminine: the caring, the love, the softness? When craving or desiring such things, we are dismissed as clingy, obsessed, crazy. The polemics on sexual liberation would often get crossed in the wires, and all I would hear was a push for sexual objectification. I couldn't enjoy sex with strangers, couldn't feel pleasure unless I was having tame, 'vanilla' sex with people I cared deeply about. Was I a prude? Was I now too much and too little at the same time?

I used to have frequent flashbacks to my abuses during sex. This was before I realised that casual or emotionless sex wasn't for me. If I didn't know the person very well, I would more often than not panic; a movement, a smell or a word reminding me of one of the twisted times. I still get flashbacks occasionally; seconds of my body being transported to a time I wish I could forget, dissociating from myself and the bedroom I'm in. I still sometimes have to stop, my partner often realising that the past has returned even before I have. Even with partners I cared for, and thus could feel pleasure with, I used to struggle to orgasm. One reason for this is inextricably tied to the fact that, as previously described, I had an orgasm during one of my previous assaults. I still carry an albatross of shame about that. If I had an orgasm, did that mean I enjoyed it? Did that mean he thought I enjoyed it? After that assault, I lied to myself for months afterwards, in denial that I had been assaulted by him. The pressure of a warped feminist sex life tried to convince me that I was being adventurous, that maybe I'd wanted to have sex with this older man and maybe I just needed to stop being so frigid about things like this. I then learned that many survivors orgasm during their assault and that doesn't negate the fact that what happened was indeed assault. An orgasm is a bodily response to genital stimulation and has nothing to do with the consent that has or hasn't been given by the person orgasming. Orgasming doesn't equal consent, and we can still be deeply traumatised in the aftermath – traumatisation then compounded by the shame we feel for physically reacting to the stimulation.

I know more confidently now what I truly desire. I desire a loving partner and caring sex. I desire kindness, connection and trust. My desires change through the days and months. Sometimes I want to be dominated. Other days I need to go slow, to let desire envelope me in tenderness. Feeling safe, calm and connected is more important than trying to prove ourselves as adventurous. Yet there's always room for complexity. If kinkiness is what you so desire, that's totally fine too. Some people who enjoy being dominated say they like it because it lets them relinquish control. Instead of relinquishing control, I personally feel like being dominated lets me gain control. I let these dominating things be done to me because I truly want them. Consensual dominance is a world apart from non-consensual dominance. Being dominant myself in sex can be intimidating, as it makes me feel like I'm risking being harmful in the situation. My past experiences have confused my own sexual assertiveness with sexual violence. I become scared that I'm being aggressive and harmful. For weeks afterwards, I worry that I did something wrong. Desire becomes synonymous with violence. How could I have acted like those men from my past? Every time I felt dominant desire, I felt wrong and dirty. Like I didn't have the right to desire someone so much; that I should only exist as an object, not an actor, of desire. This comes through most pointedly in non-heteronormative sex; my body becoming confused in the different movements, feelings and touches. I felt inexperienced and like I was purely replicating hetero-sexual sex, not making room for the fact that queer sex is beautifully different, its own world of pleasure.

This chapter has been all about having sex, but it is also radical to not have sex; to refuse the erotic and the sexuality we are told we must have. It is radical to do with your body whatever you feel is right. Trauma can affect your sex drive, as can the medications we're often put on to deal with the ongoing effects of trauma. It is normal to move in and out of your sexuality. Some weeks, I can't stop thinking about sex, can't stop fantasising about my partner; other weeks, I can't fathom being a sexual being at all, feel totally uninterested in any passion. I oscillate between feeling disgusting, steeped in shame for my sexuality, and feeling beautiful and erotic, eager for my partner to touch me. If you can't orgasm, or you only have sex once a week, or once a year, or not at all, there's nothing 'wrong' with you. Survivors shouldn't feel the need to prove their reclamation of sex to anyone. Part of me wishes I could be the liberated, sex-positive, feminist survivor I think the world wants to see. But I'm not always sex-positive. Perhaps I'm more inclined to sex-neutrality: sometimes sex can be beautiful, sometimes it can be shitty, sometimes it can be triggering. It's not supremely important for me to write about my personal sex life here. I refuse the demands set upon survivors that we must reclaim our sexualities. Sometimes, sex is just sex. It is fine, it is nice, it is uninspiring, it is amazing, it is boring. It doesn't have to be the kinkiest, best sex we've ever had, whether alone or partnered, but it's just what it is – healthy, normal sex. Because normal sex is whatever any of us is having; everything and nothing is normal sex.

# Chapter 10

# On Needing Each Other

Many posts on social media tell us we need to love ourselves first. That we need to stay single and happy and get a vibrator from a specific online store, not that they've been sponsored or anything. And, of course, the most important tenet we must follow: that we can only love someone else once we've learned how to love ourselves. In my opinion, this is all, for the most part, bullshit. Sure, self-esteem and self-worth are important in all our lives. It's wonderful if you have self-love and self-confidence, especially in a world that tries to tell you that you should hate your current self. But it's also OK to want to be loved and to want to have intimacy. Even if you don't love yourself, or indeed can't love yourself for the way you've been led to see yourself, you deserve to be loved. You don't have to wait to reach that perhaps impossible goal of self-adoration. To be a 'strong' woman, to wholeheartedly love yourself, is great if that's what's working for you. But perceived 'weakness' has its own place too. Enforced emotional resilience of the 'strong woman' is a ploy we've been taught to put up with the terrible things we have to endure in our lives. This enforced stereotype falls even harder on Black women and femmes and other women of colour. What about all the weak women: the insecure, the depressed, the lonely, the desperate? What about the people who hate everything about themselves? The false dichotomy of emotional strength and weakness, in people across the gender spectrum, is one based on ableism: that to be weak is wrong, inferior, shameful. It's also one based on misogyny: that any weak feminine trait is to be overcome or avoided altogether. But this space of 'weakness' is the one I wish to inhabit; the space of vulnerability and sensitivity. The antonym for vulnerability shouldn't have to be safety – we should be able to find safety in our vulnerability, in our humanity.

Humans are relational in nature. Social support, belonging and care is a biological necessity; we need them to survive. Love and care for oneself on an individual level should only be a partial goal within a wider goal of community care and interdependence. Self-worth is of course important in maintaining a stable internal life. But what if we struggle to love ourselves because of a previous abusive relationship, one where someone we loved told us we were worthless? What if we have an anxiety disorder, and believe that everyone hates us because we're an awful, selfish person? Behind the self-love mask we see touted on social media is often a neoliberal, capitalist ploy for us to only focus on ourselves as opposed to our community — to buy that outfit, that skincare product, to only put ourselves first. We need to care for one another, and it's OK that we need people sometimes, or indeed all the time. I'm not talking about codependency, which I won't go in to here (though it certainly can be an issue at times). I'm talking about collective care – needing a friend you can always turn to or needing a partner who you can cry to when you struggle to get through the night. All people – survivors or otherwise – deserve company and care. It shouldn't be so radical to acknowledge that. In *The Red Parts*, Maggie Nelson cites Eileen Myles: 'Need each other as much as you can bear, everywhere you go in the world.' The world is painful, the world is dark and confusing in the hellfire of the twenty-first century. So, need people, love people. Allow yourself to depend on others and to have them depend on you. It's the only way through it all.

I've had many unhealthy attachments to people throughout my life. Crushes turned into love turned into obsessions. I had a sweet, innocent love with my first boyfriend, but every relationship after that became more and more tumultuous. I was mentally ill and extremely jealous, they were all boy–men trying to navigate the weirdness of the world, and having an undiagnosed, misdiagnosed, traumatised, mentally ill girlfriend couldn't have been too easy for them (it definitely wasn't easy for me). As the years continued, my tendency to become anxiously attached to lovers became stronger.

A few years ago, I learned about something called attachment theory, first proposed in the 1950s by a psychoanalyst called John Bowlby. Essentially, Bowlby theorised that our social attachment style is formed as young children in the relationships with our caregivers. There are four attachment types: anxious (preoccupied), avoidant (dismissive), disorganised (fearful–avoidant) and

the seemingly mythical secure. Across all of my interpersonal relationships, I can flit around between all four.
My anxious attachment, however, has displayed most
obviously as preoccupation with people I'm romanti-
cally involved with – I can't stop thinking about them,
worrying obsessively about something I've done wrong; I
become terrified of real and perceived rejection, I ignore
my own needs to please the object of my affection.

I have now, thankfully, learned that attachments can
be healthy, especially when it's with beloved friends with
whom I've always had healthy relationships. I won't
go further in depth into attachment theory here, but
it's worth looking into for a further understanding of
interpersonal relationships in the aftermath of trauma,
especially childhood trauma. Since discovering myself as a
largely anxiously attached human, I've stopped negatively
labelling myself as 'too much' or 'too intense'.

During the writing of this book, I decided it was a
good idea to get a puppy. Reader, it is not a good idea
to get a puppy upon writing one's first book. Adopting
this beautiful little animal was the first insight I gained
into the mind of an avoidantly attached person (essentially,
someone who deals with their interpersonal insecurities
by not wanting anything to do with the cause of the
insecurity). I brought her home and was immediately hit
by the grief of responsibility for a living being. What the
fuck had I done? I couldn't leave the room, couldn't even
go to the loo without her crying for me to come back
to her. It was like going on a single date with someone
and having them knocking on your door for the next
week to tell you they love you, begging you not to

leave them. Unlike a human date, however, she was a dog, and she didn't know what she was doing – she was afraid and alone in a new environment. I'd wanted a dog for so long, a companion to help me through my emotional volatility in life, so when I got her and didn't know how to love her, I felt evil. My trauma response had been triggered immensely – why hadn't I heard of this before becoming a dog owner myself?

I saw too much of myself in her, saw the inner child I had so long been avoiding. I saw her raw, uninhibited reactions to life; her crying and her growling, her playfulness and her desperation for my love. It was too much, and I wanted her to leave, wanted to leave her. Is she what I'm like when I'm in love, when I'm dependent on people? I'd always considered myself a giving, loving person. She made me question my conceptions about myself – was I actually extremely selfish? Did I not know how to truly, unconditionally love another being? As the days passed and we settled into our shared life together, the love grew stronger and the bond solidified. I realised she needs me, and that is the end of it. She is not manipulative or codependent in the ways our human terms would pathologise her; she is simply a dog and I am her human. We wake up together, we spend our days together, she sleeps beside me. When I am ill, she stays by my side. I feel safer with her in my life, even though she is the size of a cat, so can offer little when it comes to actual physical protection. After stubbornly looking after myself for so long, I'm finally learning how to accept such immediately close vulnerability, finally allowing myself to open up and truly share my inner world with another being. She'll keep teaching me these overwhelmingly basic truths, as she lays in my lap as I write these words.

My phone wallpaper is a Jenny Holzer quote: *It is in your self-interest to find a way to be very tender.* It reminds me of the most sacred, central quality I want to strive towards: neither success nor confidence, honesty or clarity; simply tenderness. Tenderness for life, tenderness for my friends and my loved ones, tenderness for my dog, and tenderness for myself. I've always had close friends, friends I knew everything about and shared beds with. Yet to a certain degree, these friends were kept at arm's length. I didn't know who I was myself, didn't know how to process the secrets deep inside me, so I didn't know how to let them in. My best friend at fourteen, who is still my best friend, was the first friend I remember telling about my childhood abuse. We sat on her bedroom floor at 3 a.m. and I cried in her lap. She was one of the first people I truly let in. A few years later and I was at my first university, the one I dropped out of, and I made one beautiful friend who has still persisted despite the years, distance and minor fallouts. He saved my life, quite literally. A year after I met him, I met more loves of my life: my best friends and my chosen family. We grew up into our adulthoods together, living in London and becoming ourselves. I slowly told them about my history, the things I'd been through. And they shared the things that had happened to them too. We became family, water as thick as blood. Maybe that will change over the years, but I like to think not. Queer, femme friendship tends to stick harder than others; it's a tough and beautiful stain to budge. I learned to cry in front of them, learned to be honest and work through conflict. I learned to laugh with them until my stomach hurt. I learned what it was to be part of a healthy, requited love. Platonic love changed the way I saw love itself. I still struggle with romantic love, still struggle with trust issues, but my best friends have shown me what truly trusting another human can mean. It's a call in the middle of the night, a text that says, 'you are my favourite person', massaging one another, plaiting each other's hair, listening when we say no and holding one another when we're in pain. Always being there, no matter the distance, time or the weirdness of young life in the twenty-first century.

As Amy Berkowitz wrote, 'there's a unique kind of closeness you feel with someone after you compare experiences of sexual violence.' You may only have met that person on one random evening two years ago, but when you compare the scars of sexual trauma, you feel connected to them in ways incomparable to those who haven't experienced this specific turmoil. There's an even more intense connection you feel with fellow survivors of childhood sexual abuse. It's an alien world that seems impossible to convey to those who haven't seen it. It's like trying to describe a colour that they can't physically see; we're the mantis shrimp of traumatic experiences. No matter how I try to convey my feelings to my loved ones who aren't survivors, no matter how much I've talked about it on my podcast, there's only so far descriptions can go. Empathy and sympathy are assuredly invaluable and so desperately needed for our survival in this world, but shared experience is the most sacred form of healing

I've found. The body keeps the score, so only other bodies who know that same game can truly understand. We are united in our past pains; united in the ripping, aching inner world we've lived within since childhood. There's an undercurrent of understanding, words don't even really have to be spoken. It could simply be a brief retelling, even a look, a nod, a 'me too'.

# Chapter 11

# A Short Word on Forgiveness
*Or, why I shouldn't have to let go of my anger for a world that continues to hurt me*

'Forgiveness, as it turns out, is not a linear project. Neither is healing. Both flare up and die down.'
Esmé Weijun-Wang, *The Collected Schizophrenias*

I do not believe in forgiveness; I think it is a pointless sentiment at the best of times, a violent one at the worst. I do not forgive the people who abused me. I don't know if I ever will, at least not in the way we're conventionally told to forgive. In our religious and post-religious societies, we are told that forgiveness is the way forward; that forgiveness is the ultimate goal towards our own salvation. In the media we consume, we see TV characters in programmes telling us that forgiveness isn't about the person who harmed us but is instead about freeing ourselves from the pain of anger. But what is this fear of anger? Where is the acknowledgement that we have a right to be angry, that it is healthy to be angry in response to our harm?

The problem with forgiveness seems to be that it's misrepresented and has been mis-sold to us. I look up *Psychology Today* and it tells me that forgiveness isn't a forgetting or a return to a placid relationship with the person who has harmed you. In reality, though, the concept of forgiveness has always seemed like an oppressive force to me, has felt like another way to shut down victim–survivors – or more aptly, to shut them up. When I hear someone mention forgiveness in regard to sexual violence, for example forgiving your abuser, I feel my heckles go up. There is a special space in my chest that I reserve for the anger I have surrounding enforced forgiveness. Survivors, historically feminised, are often expected to be forgiving. If we're women, we're expected to be our nurturing, understanding, caring selves. We're told to be the bigger person; bigger than those who harmed us. It's weaponised against us, used to guilt us into sweeping the pain under the carpet. We ourselves become the carpets they use to sweep everything under, walking all over us to add insult to injury.

So, I ask, what could forgiveness look like to someone who has so long despised it? What if I want to hold onto the anger? To write it again feels good: I do not forgive my abusers. In trying to relearn what 'forgiveness' is (although I'm still unsure I'll ever be able to stomach that loaded word), perhaps it's better to think of it in terms of transformative justice. The idea of transformative justice, which I will delve deeper into later in the book, makes plenty of room for ambivalence. I do not forgive my abusers and I accept that I may never forgive them. I am always angry at them, and that anger drives me. But, at the same time, I can also understand the explanations for why they acted in such violent and harmful ways. I can hope for them to recover and grow out of their abusive tendencies for the benefit of themselves and everyone they interact with. The latter point doesn't mean that I have to forgive then. These seemingly conflicting feelings I have can exist together. I can exist in the liminal space in the middle of that Venn diagram.

Another problem I have with forgiveness, perhaps even with this new transformative conception, is that it still always feels final – like you're supposed to have completed it. Even if we're not calling it forgiveness, if it's a process of moving on and acknowledging the anger and hurt, it doesn't feel like there's any space for regression. It's not acknowledged that forgiveness can be fluid; you can feel like you've forgiven someone one day, and the next fall back into anger and resentment. In my experiences, I have only ever experienced intermittent forgiveness in relation to sexual violence. The way that I 'fall back' into anger and rage, when I have previously thought I've forgiven or 'got over' my abuse, steeps me in yet another form of shame. You feel bad, feel evil, because you can't forgive them – at least not wholly, at least not in the way you've been told forgiveness should look. We need to change our timeframe around forgiveness, ascribe to it a survivor-time. We can retract our words of forgiveness, un-forgive someone (though spellcheck tells me 'unforgive' isn't even a word), allow for its messy non-linearity.

Yet sometimes, the problem swings the other way. If I have allowed someone who has harmed me to drip back into my life on my own terms, I hear 'I hate him so much', 'How can you spend time with him?' from the mouths of my loved ones. These sentiments make my stomach sink. I feel wrong, like I've betrayed myself. Are my friends right? Am I perverted for even thinking of allowing them near me? We shouldn't force someone to forgive their abusers, but if they do forgive them, we also shouldn't force them to feel ashamed about such forgiveness or healing.

Our routes of forgiveness are no one's business but our own. This concept that forgiveness isn't about the abuser but is rather about allowing space for yourself to be free from anger is seen frequently in survivor circles. I, however, have never felt freed by forgiveness. I have felt forced, restrained from feeling my fullest embodied rage. A radical reimagining is needed towards the concept of forgiveness. What would forgiveness look like if it could be different for each person? If it was allowed as a subjective notion, a subjective feeling? Like different gods around the world, what if forgiveness could change between people, places, spaces and times? I don't want to forgive or forget. My body can never forget the harm that occurred. It can change, adapt, heal and live, but it can't forget.

# 5

# Justice

# Chapter 12

# The Criminal Justice System

I only reported the most recent one out of the four of my major sexual assaults to the police. The first sexual abuse happened when I was a child in complicated circumstances. The second two happened abroad, meaning I would have had to engage with a foreign justice system, rinsing my time and money to pursue justice that certainly wasn't guaranteed. The aftermath of the fourth assault coincided with the #MeToo movement, and I was moved to report it, thinking this was the 'right' thing to do. There are a few websites that try to objectively explain what will occur for those who haven't previously gone through reporting sexual assault to the police, but they always leave out the intense intricacies and violences that occur throughout. I reported it to the Metropolitan Police in London in 2018, and it is worth noting that the procedures mentioned will vary depending on the place and time.

I do not support this country's violent and prejudicial criminal justice system, but as it's the main form of justice we've got, let's have a quick dive into the statistical realities of the system. Many of us have heard the statistics about rape prosecutions in recent years, but they can never be repeated too often. They always struggle to completely sink in. Rape charges, prosecutions and convictions have all fallen to their lowest in a decade, despite reports rising. In the year ending March 2020, 99 per cent of rapes reported to the police in England and Wales resulted in no legal proceedings. In 2017–20, cases referred by police to the Crown Prosecution Service (CPS) to go to trial were down by 40 per cent. There were only 1,925 convictions for rape in 2018–19, despite there being 57,882 rape claims. In 2018–19, only 3.8 per cent of sexual offences resulted in a charge or court summons, down from 5.6 per cent the year before, again despite reports of sexual assault rising. The reasons for this? None have directly been given, but many various reasons are assumed: from budget cuts, a lack of referrals by the police to the CPS for prosecution, and even specific training advising prosecutors to purposefully drop certain 'grey area' cases in an attempt to improve the appearance of successful prosecution rates.

I was assaulted at the start of 2017, and the morning after it happened, I called a Rape Crisis hotline. I'm sure their hotline has helped plenty of people struggling in the aftermath of a rape, but all I remember was how awkward I felt, how I felt like I had to fill the silence and avoid being patronised. Perhaps also subconsciously afraid of seeking help, I hung up before any was substantially given and set out on a few months of solitary trauma, pain and shame.

During these months, I frequently checked the man's social media. I used to kid myself that I did this monitoring to keep myself safe, when it was really a symptom of hypervigilance along with a certain amount of self-harm. Upon one of these routine checkings, this man unknowingly prompted his own demise. It was the era of #MeToo; women everywhere had started talking, and accordingly, lots of awareness and fundraising events were being organised. I scanned his posts and, to my disbelief, saw that he was helping out with a rape charity fundraiser. My body went into overdrive. I laughed in shock, then started shaking and sobbing. I went into my flatmate's room and we spat flames over the audacity of this man. This was the final straw in the aftermath, after which I decided to report the assault to the police. His brief link to the rape-charity fundraiser had been successful in one respect: I was one of the many who felt empowered enough to try to do something, to speak up about his assault against me. So, in late 2017, I visited The Havens, a specialist rape crisis centre in London. I first rang up late on an October evening. They asked me to come in the next week to meet with some advocates.

I went in a week later with my then-partner to meet a rape victim advocate (I'll call her Vicky). I say advocate, but I can't really remember her official role – all I know is that she helped me. I sat in the waiting room in South London, right next to the library where I studied for my summer university exams and drank a weak latte from the surprisingly fancy coffee machine. Then, after a short wait, I was taken into a carpeted room with children's toys (a quietly tragic sight commonly seen in these sorts of spaces). I talked to Vicky about what the man had done to me half a year before. She was patient and kind, and she was tough. She wasn't floaty or therapist-esque, wasn't spewing the usual forced-out phrases in response to my pain. She had a dull red case file with an anonymised case number plastered across the top, which I realised must have been for me.

I can't remember many details from this time. It was a time of bottles of wine in the evening and crying alone in my room to make it through to tomorrow. It was a time of isolation and fear. In the room with the children's toys, Vicky wrote things down in the file. When I told her about my self-harm and dangerous coping mechanisms, she promised she'd tell my doctors. Not a lot of the promises that have been made to me in mental healthcare came true, but Vicky kept her promise. The doctors may not all have followed up afterwards, but she still told them nonetheless. We arranged for me to return a few days later, when I would have a chat with the police. I left into the October sunshine and went to my favourite Italian cafe nearby. What was once a relaxing revision spot had now become my refuge. I became good friends with the people who worked there. There was some gentle comfort in chatting banally about coffee and cake every week after sobbing in front of rape therapists or the police just moments prior.

A few days later, I returned to The Havens, via a stressful journey with my partner on a slow-service South London bus. The stress was excruciating; I was so paranoid we'd be late, even though we ended up being half an hour early. The report was something I decided I needed to do alone, so my partner reluctantly waited at the Italian cafe again. I was adamant that doing it alone was something I must do to protect myself. Something told me that as I was alone when it happened, I must be alone to see it through to the end. Would I allow someone in with me if I were seeking help today? Would I let my current partner, or my mum, help me now? I'm unsure. I hate to still feel allegiance to the stoicism I saw as necessary for my survival then.

I waited with Vicky again in the small, eerily comfortable room. There were the children's toys again. Little looping structures with blocks, like those I used to play with at the shoe shop or the bank when I was a child waiting for my mum to run her errands. Were these toys there for children who'd been harmed, or were they there to distract them when their carers, mothers, fathers were being helped? Perhaps many children were there for both reasons. The world can be a sad place. Whilst I thought about this, Vicky explained to me what would happen in the meeting with the police. I was reminded that it wasn't a formal statement, but an initial reporting.

I was then brought into another room where my 'special police officer', let's call her Nicole, was. Someone else was there too, another police officer or maybe someone in training. It was another woman, as I asked for only women on my case, but I can't remember this other woman at all; she is just a faceless body in the corner of my memory. Vicky was with me too, a silent protector, although she couldn't do much protecting in this situation. I had brought with me a written account of what happened. I had taken this account from what I had written in a journal the morning after the assault happened. I then told the officers what happened, my full account, without reading from the written one at all. I secretly thought this would make me more credible – the fact that I knew my story from memory and that it was also written down, like learning a presentation off by heart at school. Two pieces of evidence supporting my reliable truth-telling. I also told them about the original diary entry from the morning after my assault (a third piece of truth).

They wrote down this report, took my written account, and asked practical questions (there was no cross-examination at this time). They asked where it happened, what time, if there were any secondary witnesses (those who were in the house at the same time, or those who had seen me directly afterwards). They asked for details of the perpetrator, so they could find him. They explained that I would next have to provide a formal witness statement. You are your own primary witness in a case of assault; the key witness to your own rape.

Afterwards, I again went into the sunlight, went to my Italian cafe, went home. It was Halloween. I slept and watched films I now have no recollection of. I missed a Halloween party, my body too tired. I drank wine. I slept.

My memories have calcified since all this took place. When I first wrote about this experience on my website, I was timid and careful in my description of this process. I didn't want to put people off reporting if they were considering it. I am still tentative, afraid to so gravely influence a significant moment in a survivor's life. Yet, I continue with my story.

A week or two later – time blurs thick in these memories – I gave my statement. The witness statement can

either be given as a video or a written statement. I opted
to do the video statement, the one recommended by all
the officials for the fact that it takes a shorter amount of
time to collect. It took place at a South London Police
Station, because my statement needed to be given in the
borough where the assault had happened. It took an hour
to travel there, and my partner was with me, comforting
me. During the interview, she waited for me somewhere
nearby, unable to come in with me (although I would
likely have declined, even if she were allowed to). Nicole
met me outside, took me in through to the statement
room. I briefly met the case detective, a blonde woman
in a suit. She sat in the 'control room' next door, where
she'd be recording the CCTV footage on a DVD.

The interview was awful. Yes, they may try to make
it as 'nice' for a victim as possible, but how nice can it
be to recount your trauma in a police station – a site
of so much violence and fear? The 'comfort suite' was
beige and grey. Maybe the furniture was coloured, like
the sort of mottled colourings used on bus or tube seats
to hide the dirt, but in my memory it's dull. There were
children's toys, again alluding silently to some awfulness.
Nicole showed me that there were CCTV cameras in
the room, recording everything. I was told when they'd
started recording me. I was to give my statement of
events, exactly as they occurred on that night. I took
off my shoes and clung to a jumper I had brought
with me, even though it was too hot in the room. As
I recounted the night, she asked questions, so many
questions, throughout: '*Were your clothes on or off?*', '*How
many beers had he had?*', '*And you let him stay?*' I couldn't

finish a sentence without a question being asked. It was a gruelling, traumatising two hours of reliving the night I so wished to forget. It was a trick mirror of trauma reprocessing therapy, without the actual support and aim of gentle reprocessing. It branded the night into my head.

It is a fuzzy and sour memory, that statement room. It made me realise Nicole was not on my side. She may have thought she was, mostly acted as if she was, but there was one precise moment that broke the façade. She clarified at the beginning of the interview that she would have to ask some difficult questions, for if the case went to trial, the defence would ask such questions anyway. She said that if we 'got them out of the way' in the statement, it'd be much easier. I don't know what's easier: being doubted out loud in court by the defence team, who are paid to defend your rapist, an experience that is horrible, cruel and damaging but can be rationalised quite easily, or being doubted out loud by the person supposed to help you, indeed seeing their doubt pour out of them so naturally. After I'd recounted the night, Nicole asked, '*Do you think you may have been leading him on?*' The memory punches me in the gut, reverberates around my head, just as it did back then. Yet I had to play it cool, had to answer immediately, show no signs of doubt or worry. How is that a question a survivor is supposed to answer? *Oh yes, gosh, Nicole, you're right after all! I was just leading him on . . . how silly of me!*

As I look over the law regarding sexual assault, I read the Metropolitan Police's definitions of sexual violence. I see the subheading, 'You are not to blame'. This was not the impression I got when, in my recorded interview, my officer asked me such a question. This was also not the impression I got when a friend of mine was told that the fact she had invited her rapist over before the assault occurred meant that her case wasn't being taken forward, nor the impression I got when my friend's skirt length was used as evidence to insinuate she was to blame for her rape.

This question made me freeze, made me solid in the room, just as his hands had done half a year before. My body went into a trauma response again − I felt dissociated, made the motions, but didn't really feel that what was happening was real. I felt completely alone in the world, isolated from anything I thought I knew. But I survived it, just as I had survived him. It makes me feel sick to think that they still have those DVDs of me in the interview room − but that they also have the interview videos of him. The discs are most likely in the same file, stuck together somewhere, forgotten in a dusty cupboard in a police station; the physical closeness of them is torturous.

When you complete the statement-giving, you sign some forms consenting to their use in the investigation. I have no idea what those forms said, but I must have signed them. How are you supposed to read through your rights when you have just been re-traumatised only seconds before? You sign yourself away because there's no other option. Rushing out, trying to leave the trauma behind (though I was just at the beginning of processing it), my partner and I ate in Brixton Market. We then watched a gore-filled horror film in Peckhamplex cinema; showing again how violence and normality exist side by side, constantly. Some days you just feel it more.

During this next stage, the police collect statements from others involved with the crime. If you have witnesses to the crime, or if you told someone directly afterwards, then you will be asked to provide their details so the police can contact them, and they will be asked to give witness statements. These witnesses, however, do not have to provide a statement. My best friends were contacted; they had to give their accounts of what I'd told them and how I'd acted directly afterwards, to see if our 'stories matched'. My best friend had to recount, second-by-second, how I called her the morning after, told her she needed to come over, cried in her arms. How I told her what had happened, and she stayed with me the whole day, trying to hold me together as I fell apart, too afraid to be left alone. The evening after, there was a party and some of my friends were going out. Only two of them knew what had happened the night before. The group had pre-drinks at the house I shared with friends, as I sat with them in a haze of fatigue and confusion. Afterwards, I lay in my flatmate's bed and cried myself to sleep.

It was around this time that I found out my rapist admitted that he was 'kissing me and didn't stop' (. . . so let's look at this logically) and that something had elusively 'happened' with me. Did he know what he did? Did he know how much he'd broken me?

The accused was also to be contacted at this stage. If they have previous charges on their record, the accused will be arrested and brought in for questioning. If it's a first formal offence they will be asked to come in for questioning, but if they refuse or leave during the questioning they can and will be arrested. They will then be released on caution. They will be told not to make any contact with you, either personally or through a third party; for instance, asking one of their friends to contact you. If they do so, you can tell the police who will tell them again not to contact you. If they do so again, you can get a restraining order against the perpetrator/s of this harassment. I wonder what it was like for him, being asked to go in. Was he shocked? Was he scared? Did he care? We would have walked through the same doors, seen the same people. Did he think about what it was like for me?

The stage that follows is one of evidence-collecting, which may take several months. If you went to the hospital and had a rape kit collected, this will be tested in labs, a process which can take a long time, especially in places like London – I've heard of times ranging between four and nine months, possibly longer. If evidence is successfully found, this will be used in the investigation. I did not have a rape kit tested. I didn't go to the police immediately after I was assaulted, so I missed the required time frame of seventy-two hours for accurate DNA testing. Although I knew that what had happened to me was wrong, I didn't think I wanted to go to the police about it. It was something I wanted to deal with alone. I also don't believe I was seriously physically injured, so my trauma may have been invisible, unprovable, anyway. A test of my body and my bedsheets would have proven the accused was in my house, my room, and that he had touched my body. But the abuse I had suffered mightn't have been told in those sheets, in my underwear or on my skin. After learning about these processes, abuse can make you hyperaware of your body in this world—all the germs and pieces of DNA constantly floating around you.

A few years ago, after the assault, I had piss thrown at me from a stranger's car whilst I was kissing a girl on a busy London road. When I returned home later on that night, drunk and enraged, I went into autopilot and yanked off a piece of my hair, rubbed a cotton swab over my face and scalp. I knew the piss-thrower's DNA was quite definitely on me, and I knew that if I ever wanted to do anything about it in any official capacity, I would need the DNA as evidence. I never reported that attack, yet I still have the evidence collected at the back of my bathroom cupboard. It lays there, floating DNA as a reminder of hate mixed in with my own tenacious attempt to protect myself.

Other evidence, such as text messages and other data from phones, and rape counselling notes if you received counselling directly from a crisis centre, can be used in the investigation. You can consent not to provide this evidence, or to partially omit certain things, but the police do recommend that you give consent to full access for the sake of 'complete transparency'. They urge complete transparency from the already traumatised victim. We have to give our whole lives over to prove to them that we were harmed as we said we were. This is why we repeat over and over the necessity to believe women, believe survivors. We shouldn't have to spread our blood on the walls just to prove our hurt.

My phone was taken from me for six months. It was lucky that I had access to another phone that I could still use in my everyday life. Other women, however, aren't so lucky; women like Katrina O'Hara, whose mobile was taken by the police for investigation after she reported her ex-lover, Stuart Thomas, for domestic abuse and harassment in 2016. Eight days after her phone was taken, she was brutally murdered by Stuart Thomas. As she had no phone, she had no means of calling for help. She was a mother of three and she mattered. The officers in this case were found at fault for misconduct, for not properly considering the seriousness of the circumstances. After her murder, they were only reprimanded with management advice and a written warning. She might be alive had they done their job to help her, or had she simply had a phone to call for help.

I often wonder what they did with my phone in the time they had it. They scraped it for data, I know that much – many refer to it as a 'digital strip search'. But what data did they strip? Why did they need it for six months? Why can't I know what they took, why didn't they inform me? Did they see the photos of my friends and me, the pictures I took travelling with my first love the summer before, the pictures of my childhood dog who'd recently died? Did they read private jokes with my best friends, the nudes I had taken for myself and for lovers? This old phone still lies at the bottom of my electronics storage box under my bed, its blue case no doubt flecked with remnants of the police station's atmosphere.

I know that they didn't take his phone as a part of the investigation, or at least not until the very end. My phone was taken in May, right at the beginning of the investigation. No attempt was made to take his phone until the end of September, five months later. How was it for him to have the privilege of digital privacy for all those months I wasn't granted it? Would they have taken the same amount of data from him? Would they have scoured his texts for evidence of a joke he may have made or to see where he was the day after the assault occurred? Was he at home, in the midst of a breakdown, unable to face the world, too?

I could, with a large pinch of salt, see why they would want to see the text conversations both before and after an assault to support basic details being told by those involved. Where my cautious acceptance ends is in the fact that it's not just our correspondences with the accused that get examined by the police. In London, the Metropolitan Police can (and do) pull your message records, call records, your photos, videos, social-media records, emails, apps, web-browsing data, deleted data. This collected data can be kept for one hundred years. It's highly likely that these searches infringe on our data-protection and privacy rights: Big Brother Watch estimates that each investigation seeks 30,000 pages of information from a victim. Understandably, one out of five survivors refuse to give their phone over for the intrusive evidence collection. It was found that in every case of refusal, the case was subsequently dropped by the investigators. There's a postcode lottery with this, though – in some areas, they demand these large swathes of data, in others they demand no such digital data, showing that it's largely an arbitrary procedure, which makes it all the more cruel. If a case then makes it to court, the defence will be given the evidence, including this digital evidence, to sift through and use to discredit victims. They can pick apart the texts you sent to the accused before the assault took place; the ones where you asked him to come over could be used to twist the jury's mind that you were asking for what was done to you: *do you think you may have been leading him on?*

We have no way of knowing the plethora of data they have taken from our phones, unless we ask after the case is dropped or completed. If we defend our data rights, refusing to hand over our valuable digital life, we are denied justice. In the writing of this chapter, a lot of feelings and fears were raised about the process I went through. A repressed fear about my data came to the surface. I allowed myself to realise that the Met Police still have a large amount of data on me, locked away somewhere in a warehouse. Since new UK General Data Protection Regulation laws had since come in, I figured I may stand a chance in getting some of my data removed. After consulting with Big Brother Watch, I enquired with my police officer, Nicole, about having all irrelevant data they'd acquired from my phone deleted. I wasn't even talking about having *all* of my data deleted, as I knew they would have to keep some of it in case the investigation was reopened. Nicole responded to my query quickly: they couldn't do what I'd asked because all of my data is apparently stored in a secure warehouse, in the investigation case file, for thirty years. Thirty years. She told me that if I wanted to, I could formally request to know what data they held on me – I had a right to that. But did I really want to know what they had on me if there was no chance that I could ask for it to be deleted? Did I really want to see what they viewed as potential evidence of my lying? After a short exchange of emails, Nicole tried to reassure me: she'd looked, and it didn't look like there'd been any evidence of use from the phone anyway. Impossibly, this crushed me further. Her words of reassurance were a final kick – they'd had my phone for six months, and they still held an unknown amount of data on me, but not to worry, because it was all useless anyway. I filled out a data subject access request to the Met Police. I went to print it, and something else got in the way. When I later remembered the form, I cringed at the thought of printing it. I decided I would not go through this process; would not subject myself further to the violent bureaucracy of their systems. I have to make peace, knowing they'll hold such private information about me until I'm fifty-one.

If all of the above wasn't bad enough, it somehow gets worse. After The Havens had helped me report my assault to the police, they offered me free and immediate rape counselling. It seems that this counselling was what's known as 'pre-trial therapy', although I was still at the stage of investigation prior to knowing whether the case would go to trial. It's now time to tell you that The Havens is co-run by the NHS and the Metropolitan Police. In the therapy they provide, I was told that I wasn't allowed to talk about the rape. Naturally then, whilst attending, I asked what the point of it was. My therapist tried to assure me that I could talk about my feelings around it, my emotions. Yet I was told that I must constrain myself, must watch what I said. The reason for this, I was explicitly told, was because the police could ask for my counselling notes, which they did, and if the case went to trial, the defence could use what I'd said against me. I was told that I could deny giving them the counselling notes, but if I did so, it was likely my case would be dropped.

My therapist offered me the opportunity to look through my counselling notes and block out anything I didn't want them to see or know, but again, it was reiterated that this may look 'suspicious' to the police or the defence. Looking back, I wish I had reviewed the notes, omitted my personal pains and trauma, my insides, from the cruel eyes of the law. But I don't blame myself for not doing so. I was so tired, so drained from everything, that I couldn't face reading over the typed-up recordings of my emotional fallout. I told her they could use it all. I was exhausted. I'm still exhausted.

The police can also demand your medical records. I can see from my medical records that they did indeed do this in my case. I only found this out through research for this book. Upon discovering this fact, I felt both deep pain and deep apathy. I wonder what they would have used against me. My history of mental illness or my previous child sexual abuse? Both, I expect. How can we process such deep violations? How can we carry this unspeakable anger?

During the process of writing this chapter, the UK police announced a scrapping of both the digital strip-searching process and a recalling of the use of therapy notes in rape investigations. I wait to see what they will be replaced with, but fear little will substantially change. Even if the official policy changes, the culture of disbelief and the use of victim–survivors' private materials will still likely be enforced on local levels. My fears were confirmed when I read the official line from the police, clarifying these proposed scraps: 'police and prosecutors have a duty to pursue all reasonable lines of inquiry in every investigation'. My question therefore is: what is 'reasonable'? Is it reading through our therapy notes, supplying them to the defence to destroy us in court? Is it keeping our phones for months on end, even when no substantive evidence could be found? Although the official procedures may have been scrapped, who's to know what each officer sees as reasonable? If officers still enforce the old rules, who will be there to stop them? A complaints procedure may exist, but I know that if I was back in that situation, the last thing I'd want to do, with what precious energy I miraculously had left, would be to file a formal complaint with the institution that had so fiercely let me down, had so deeply re-traumatised me.

A victim can withdraw their statement at any time during the investigation. This does not mean retracting it, claiming the crime didn't happen, but means that the victim's witness statement can't be used in the ongoing investigation, and therefore it won't be possible for the case to go to court. I was told that, if I withdrew my statement, I could still reopen the case at any time to continue the investigation. The accused would also be informed of the same potentiality.

In September 2018, half a year after my first report to the police, the world around me had its eyes and ears glued to the coverage of the US Senate hearing concerning Brett Kavanaugh's sexual assault allegations. Dr Christine Blasey-Ford told the world that Kavanaugh, Donald Trump's then nominated (now elected) Supreme Court Judge candidate, had sexually assaulted her when she was fifteen years old. He denied it. What happened to Dr Blasey-Ford in that hearing destroyed a large part of her life – she had to move to a new house due to the threats to her and her family's life. It would also have repercussions for survivors across the world. What happened with this case – the way his defendants spoke about her, defended his honour, said that he had been an innocent target as she was ripped to shreds for her tenacity and intelligence; the way the world reacted to it, debating and watching it as a circus show – led to me withdrawing my own statement, dropping my own police case. I saw what Blasey-Ford had to endure the way she was belittled whilst her perpetrator was defended, even glorified. It momentarily destroyed me and monumentally changed the course of my actions. I saw my potential future dramatically reflected in the horror of her gawked-at testimony to the Senate. I cried for the destruction she was facing, the anger and hate Kavanaugh was allowed to spit to draw pity from the watching world.

In the days after, I knew I couldn't go through with my case. I couldn't – wouldn't – go through what she had gone through. I knew I had to protect myself. Blasey-Ford was forced into her position – she knew the realities of the 'justice' system in the USA and yet she still tried to battle it. She herself was on trial, though she had committed no crime. She put her life on the line – quite literally, receiving death and rape threats, having to move out of her home – to try to stop her rapist becoming an overseer of the law in the country she calls home. Throughout the trial, it became clear that the problem wasn't just that her doubters didn't believe her story, it was that they didn't interpret the acts she recounted as a harmful crime. They retorted that it was 'just boys being boys'; it was 'lad culture; it was fun, it wasn't rape'. This dark performance taught me that there was a large part of the world who did not care about us or our survival. The momentum gained during the #MeToo movement felt like it was fading, misogyny taking centre stage once more.

After emailing Nicole to tell her that I wanted to withdraw my statement, to halt the investigation, she replied that it would only take half an hour of my time. Half an hour and it would all be over. Half an hour of telling them why I was withdrawing, signing a form, and after six months of an investigation, it would all be over. If only it was that simple in my own body too. It was the last time I'd be in the beige, sweated-in victim's room.

When asked why I was withdrawing my statement, I was honest with Nicole. I told her that the pressure of the case was becoming too much, that witnessing the vitriol surrounding the Kavanaugh case in the prior weeks had been a grim foreshadowing for a future I didn't want to bring myself into. To my disbelief, Nicole asked me who Brett Kavanaugh was and what Senate hearing I was speaking of. Now, of course it's tricky to stay up to date with news, I get that. I'm no expert here, but surely, if you're a special officer working with survivors of sexual violence, you should perhaps stay up to date with current contemporary affairs that could severely affect the people you are working for. Or, I don't know, perhaps it's an idea to listen to the radio or engage with some sort of news if you're working for the public-facing police force? I laughed incredulously as I had to briefly explain to her the year's biggest news point concerning sexual violence – all whilst I was ending the only attempt I'd made at seeking justice, or what I had previously thought to be 'justice'. Something tells me I made the right decision.

After any crime, victims may apply for a scheme called criminal injuries compensation, where you can be awarded compensation from the assailant for the pain and trauma caused. I was advised not to apply for any compensation, as once again it could be used against me to make it look like 'I was lying', like I was 'doing it all for money'. There's a clear pattern emerging throughout this whole process. We are told to appear a certain way, to be the 'perfect victim', to brutalise ourselves for the appearance of innocence, to give our whole selves over to them, to refrain from asking for the least amount of compensation we deserve. Sexual violence destroys lives. Many of us can't work, can't sleep, can't eat, can't go outside following such violence. Receiving compensation for these injustices is the least that could be awarded, but we are told we shouldn't be asking. We'd be the classic lying gold-digger, the bitch accusing any man of rape just to get our hands on some money or sympathy. I would ask anyone who has thought such things to read through this experience with the police, or other experiences that have seen even more severe injustices, and question why anyone would lie to the police about being a survivor of sexual violence.

There are a couple of stages to the end of an investigation. The police will collect all evidence and send the compiled case to senior detectives. These senior detectives will then decide if there is enough evidence to send the case to the CPS (Crown Prosecution Service). The CPS will then decide whether or not to take the case to court to prosecute the defendant, where a jury will decide whether the defendant is guilty or not guilty. So, there's a two-stage decision process: the semi-finals of making it through to the CPS after the detectives have assessed the case, and then the finals where the CPS will decide to take it through to trial. I never made it to this stage because I withdrew my statement before it was possible. I strongly doubt my case would have been referred to the CPS, as it was such a 'he said, she said' case. Yet, early in the investigation, I was told by Nicole that there seems to be no rhyme or reason for referral to the CPS. She said there were previous cases she'd seen with little evidence go through to trial, whilst others with overwhelming evidence had been rejected before they could even be referred to the CPS.

For many, experiences of the legal system don't end when the investigation, or the trial, does. There are laws around libel and slander – 'good' laws for many, like those who have been targeted horrifically by the UK press or have been discriminated against in some way. Libel concerns written texts harming the reputation of individuals and slander concerns spoken words doing the same. Where the laws fall short, actively harming people, is when they are used to punish those who speak out against violence they have suffered. If a case doesn't go to trial, or if jurors find the defendant 'not guilty', usually because of a lack of evidence – a conclusion overwhelmingly common – and the victim–survivor speaks out about their experience, potentially identifying the accused, then the accused may feel empowered by the lack of a criminal conviction and sue the accuser and take them to court for defamation. This is assuredly easier for some accused individuals to do, specifically those with lots of money – financial privilege goes a long way in shutting women up.

By its very nature, this chilling effect often happens silently, and leaves the victim feeling as if they have been gagged and are, unable to speak of the experience at all. It happened to Lucy and Verity Nevitt, twins who were sexually assaulted by the same man, when they spoke out about their abuse on Twitter after their police case was dropped. The accused sued them, forcing them to pay legal fees out of their own pockets until they eventually managed to find a pro-bono solicitor at the last minute. They eventually came to a settlement where the Nevitts are allowed to speak of their experience, but with an asterisk – they're never allowed to name him. It is a devastating and torturous blow, having to scrape funds together to protect themselves from their rapists' attempts to further pull them down.

This cruel tactic also leads to ricocheting preventative efforts. This can lead to those giving survivors a platform seeking to protect themselves from libel claims by asking survivors to sign a waiver before they speak of their abuse in a public context, and to put in place measures to avoid the risk of 'jigsaw identification'. This is where the public may be able to piece together who the accused is based on identifying information that could be linked together. Survivors are often told they cannot use certain words, cannot say certain things, for it would risk them being exposed to a defamation complaint – which could get them in trouble but often also, more importantly, get institutions in trouble. I know all of this because it was something my team and I had to cover with all of the guests on my BBC podcast. It's also something that will have happened in the publishing of this book, with a lawyer hired to check I haven't been libellous in any way. The institutions I've worked for are huge, world-renowned organisations, so I understand why they have to apply these measures and rules to avoid lawsuits, even if I strongly disagree with such restrictions. That doesn't mean the effects of the measures are any less damaging.

Let me first be clear that at no point in the recording of the series or the writing of this book did we want to actively accuse or call out individuals for the harms they had committed. At no point did we want to name names, or even places. That was never the point. The key point, as I hope was shown on my podcast series, was to give survivors a voice to talk about themselves, not the person who hurt them; to talk about their own feelings and how they survive to this day. One guest understandably pulled out of the series because the legal team were trying to get her to sign a document that essentially denied the rape had occurred because the accused was found 'not guilty' in court. I had another guest, 'Melissa'*, who persisted through this violent bureaucracy, determined to be on the podcast, only to be told that she had to change her name and voice (we had to use a voice actor) to tell her story of going to court and having the accused also be found 'not guilty'. Even after I begrudgingly agreed to these measures – as the guest, a friend of mine, reassured me she was willing to continue to get her story told – I was then told I couldn't even introduce her as a survivor or refer to the experience of her rape. Not only had this survivor had parts of her story omitted (for risk of identification), her name changed, her voice changed – now she wasn't even being allowed the status of survivor. This was the only time I blew up at my studio, shouting in the lobby. When I was told this protocol, that I couldn't introduce her as I had originally scripted (in line with the truth), I stood up in rage, shouting 'I fucking hate lawyers', making awkward eye-contact with a skittish man about to record his podcast about sports.

I know for a fact that, had my case gone to court (and I strongly assume the accused would have been found 'not guilty'), I would not have been able to create the podcast with the BBC. I wouldn't be able to write these very words. I probably would have been putting myself at legal risk for even creating my website. The fact I feel lucky, grateful, for dropping my case so that I could create

---

\* I implore you to listen to this episode of the podcast, Melissa's episode, to hear the abysmal realities of having a rape case go to court. It is not an easy listen, but it is an essential one.

these resources, is simply incredibly fucked. My question is: how many people can't tell their stories, have been denied their voices, because of these legal restrictions? It's not just the fact that we have to go through these horrendous experiences, it's that it's near impossible for many of us to legally discuss it after it's happened. We are gagged, both officially and unofficially, the violence continuing long after the original assault. 'Melissa' was tenacious when she shouldn't have had to be. She fought and put herself aside to get her horrendous experience of the UK Crown Prosecution Service told. How many survivors' stories go unheard, how many have tried to tell their story and been sued, or simply ignored?

There were some people I had on my potential guest list for the podcast whom I would have loved to speak with, but I was advised by numerous people in the chain of command that their stories were too 'tricky' or too 'risky' to tell on public-service radio. I had to weigh up whether I wanted to be a part of this insidious legal system, to toe the line of legal bureaucracy that a large institution demands; or whether I could create the podcast independently. I chose to go with the institution, which makes me complicit with all the things we enforced on survivors. It was not my fault that this institution was having to enforce these standard protocols on vulnerable people. Yet I did agree to enable it, because I believed that getting the podcast 'out there' on such a major platform was a resistance and a disruption in itself, and that, most importantly, we as survivors would be heard. I don't know whether it was the right decision, but was there any right decision? Had I rejected the institution, independently created the podcast (with no audio training), who would it have benefited? Myself and my morals? What about all the people who this podcast has helped? Simultaneously, what about the people who the podcast hurt, who were ignored because of the legal system that was created for our downfall? I don't know the answers. Perhaps, like so much else, there is no single answer: I can hold these multiple truths and multiple problems at once, in a confusing mess of trying to do the 'right' thing.

The system isn't broken, it is doing exactly as it is designed to: sacrificing feminised victims to maintain the innocence of socially powerful, masculine abusers. Survivors are belittled and torn apart at every corner of the justice system. These institutional experiences can be referred to as the second rape, the re-traumatisation sometimes on a par with the original violence that led us to try to find justice in the first place. Even though there may be individuals working within the system trying to make the experience of the justice system less dehumanising and traumatising for victim-survivors, they can't overpower the gargantuan system that devotes itself to the maxim of 'innocent until proven guilty'. The system will always side with the powerful, no matter what costs survivors must pay in the process.

Despite being critical of the criminal justice system, I will not shame you if you went to the police; I will not blame myself for doing so too. I won't shame you if you decide to go to the police in the future, either. I will not shame us for how we decided to try to cope at the time. In the next chapters, however, I will shine some light on the alternatives to seeking justice via the police. Alternatives that may give us some hope for a better future for survivors.

# Chapter 13

# A Brief Introduction to Transformative Justice

'I want us to do better. I want to feel like we are responsible for each other's transformation. Not the transformation from vibrant flawed humans to bits of ash, but rather the transformation from broken people and communities to whole ones.'

adrienne maree brown

Most survivors will say that they seek justice for the violence committed against their bodies. But what does justice mean, especially if it doesn't look like the criminal justice system we currently live with? Our culture is founded on crime and punishment, on vengeance. The law of retaliation is sewn into the fabrics of our societies. But instead of an eye for an eye, it's endless days in a confined space; it's social ostracisation and humiliation; it's more violence for the original violence that was committed against someone's bodily autonomy. As I've just described in the previous chapter, half a year after I was last sexually assaulted, I reported what had happened to the police. I did this because it's what I thought I was supposed to do; it 'felt' right, it felt needed, it felt urgent to prevent any further harm being committed by him against women I'd never know. I did this because after years of violence being committed against me, I thought this was the only way to fight back. I wish I knew then what I have come to understand now. I wish I knew that I wouldn't find healing or care in the current criminal justice system; that my own dignity would be stripped well before his. More than that, I wish I knew that, outside of my own personal struggles, the criminal justice system is an institution built for the purpose of oppression and disappearing the undesirables of society. This chapter is an overview of alternative concepts of justice. Many feminists have conflicting views and disagree about justice. I do not proclaim to know everything or to have definitive solutions to the problem of what to do with abusers, but instead invite you to open up a dialogue with yourself, with your community. More on this in the next chapter.

Before we get into alternative concepts of justice, I want to explore the ethos of the current system we have, the one shown from my point of view in the previous chapter. The British criminal justice system is punitive, along with all criminal justice systems across the world – we haven't reached the utopian dream anywhere just yet. It works on the basis of incarcerating those who break society's laws. Without further inspection, this will seem fair enough to many people. What isn't ruminated on or made clear by our overarching white, elite society is the insidiousness of the system – the way it works by oppressing marginalised communities and appeasing those who hold more power. 'But,' people may ask, 'what about the bad guys, what about the rapists?' The answer to this understandable worry is that most rapists aren't in prison. In fact, most people who are raped don't report it to the police. Of rapes that are reported, most won't make it to court, and then most of the ones that do will subsequently be found 'not guilty'.

Besides all this data showing that the system is broken in what it sets out to do, on a fundamental level the criminal 'justice' system seeks no real justice for either victim–survivors, perpetrators or their communities. There is no space made for accountability; no space for people to take on board the harm they've done or to work to try to rectify or repair the situation. Simply locking people up will not teach them about male supremacy, toxic masculinity, consent and why sexual violence occurs in our societies. Further, the system breeds denial and actually reinforces a lack of accountability from those who have committed harm – think of the defence attorney appointed on behalf of accused perpetrators to vehemently deny any wrongdoing. The concept of 'innocent until proven guilty' reigns supreme, with all efforts going towards maintaining innocence rather than encouraging accountability. Wealthy, powerful men are taught to sue those who accuse them in any public capacity.

We may be taught as children to say 'sorry' when we have wronged someone, but this stops suddenly in adulthood with the more grave wrongs. The current system isolates everyone, both the victim and the perpetrator. The victim–survivors are essentially put on trial, the burden of proof lying at their feet, so they have to play the 'perfect victim'. The accused perpetrators are told to deny everything, to paint the accuser as a liar, a slut, a crazy person. Victim–survivors are shamed, cross-examined in court, questioned by their police officers – *do you think you may have been leading him on?* Certain perpetrators are scapegoated: men of colour, certain cultural communities, 'creepy old men'. Victim–survivors themselves are also criminalised; 57 per cent of women in UK prison report being survivors of domestic violence, and 53 per cent of women and 26 per cent of men in prison report surviving childhood abuse. However, the charity Women in Prison estimates these figures to be even higher because many survivors fear disclosing abuse, with 79 per cent of women using their services having experienced domestic and/or sexual violence. Across the globe, survivors are incarcerated for defending themselves from abusive situations when the 'protective' state was nowhere to be seen – people like Ky Peterson, Joan Little, Cyntoia Brown and Alisha Walker (for more information on these survivors and similar cases, please google their names or search YouTube for 'Survived and Punished').

Carceral feminism, defined by Elizabeth Bernstein, is a feminism that sees criminalisation and extended incarceration of perpetrators as a way of achieving gender equity, liberation and justice. Carceral feminists campaign for more laws, more surveillance and longer sentences for those who commit crimes against women and girls. With these laws, we run away to the ultimate protective patriarch – the state – to protect us from the perceived minority of big bad monsters. The mythical perfect victim's safety is used as a tool to justify the state's racist and classist oppression, as Angela Y. Davis explains in *Women, Race and Class*. The laws created to protect this idealised person justifies punishment and shame as a way of preventing crime, adhering to a strict binary of abused and abuser. To those so inclined, this may seem like a good idea. But what carceral feminists may often leave out or skim over is everything surrounding the instances of individual sexual violence. They leave out the male supremacist culture we live in and the way it needs to be tackled from the community, bottom up, and not just with individual prison sentences. They leave out the ways in which poverty breeds intergenerational violence and the way hostile border regimes push undocumented women into survival sex work where they're more vulnerable to abuse. They leave out the way benefit cuts and the crisis of universal credit pushes women to remain in violent relationships for the sake of their own and their children's long-term survival. They leave out the way people from marginalised communities will always be more affected by increased sentences and surveillance. They think that introducing these laws and longer sentences will help, will deter perpetrators from committing crimes again, but they unfortunately don't. They just put a threadbare bandage over the gaping wound. No matter the laws put in place, people with power will always have the capacity to abuse those they have power over, because the cultural norm of violence, male supremacy and white supremacy will still remain in place. The reason sexual violence exists in our society is because of misogyny and an entitlement to certain bodies – and prisons won't make those things go away. To combat sexual violence, these things must be addressed and dismantled from the ground up.

We must also ask who is making and passing the laws. Is it the people truly affected by the violence: a queer man trying to cope with his childhood sexual abuse at the hands of his estranged father, or a woman abused as a child who recovers her memories of sexual abuse in her forties? Or is it conservative men, perhaps themselves accused of sexual violence, ruling over the most powerful states in the world? Who will the current laws punish? Those who fit the 'perfect perpetrator' stereotype, that is, men of colour and queer men? What about those like Brock Turner, the infamous white, college-educated man who received a six-month sentence for the sexual assault of Chanel Miller? The most marginalised in society will always suffer the biggest brunt of purportedly feminist laws.

What carceral feminists also fail to acknowledge is the sexual violence perpetrated within the prison system by the state. For example, of the 594 complaints of a sexual nature against London Met employees between 2012 and 2018 (*The Observer*), only 119 were upheld. Or, in cases like that of Theo Luhaka, a Black man who was sexually assaulted by police whilst being arrested in Paris, or cases where rape and sexual violence occur daily in prisons around the world – violence we see joked about casually in TV shows: *don't drop the soap*. How can we be advocates for survivors of sexual violence whilst simultaneously pushing others into vulnerable positions where they too may be forced to engage in sexual activity? This revenge isn't justice, and no one, even a rapist, 'deserves' to be raped.

Before delving into what transformative justice actually is, we must take a moment to acknowledge where it came from. Transformative justice, in everything but the term, has been used for aeons within communities that could never rely on the police and the state. Sure, I and many others may choose not to engage with the police, but many communities indeed can't call the police because they're already targeted by the state in various ways: living in fear of deportation, brutality and/or arrest because of their criminalised lines of work. Women of colour and Black communities have long been enacting forms of transformative justice in their communities and helping their peers on a journey of accountability. The ethos of transformative justice has long existed and has a legacy owed to an unquantifiable number of people in these communities, like those of INCITE!, GenerationFIVE, Philly Stands Up, Cradle Community, Sisters Uncut and The Audre Lorde Project, to name but a few. All knowledge I've gained has been formed from such communities and groups (please look them up and donate to their projects, if you're able).

As we find no healing in our current punitive justice system, what other ways could provide healing? There are two prevailing alternatives: restorative justice and transformative justice. Both of them are informed by the survivors' needs. Both of them see a path to accountability and healing, as opposed to punishment and shaming, as a way of repairing past harms and preventing future ones from occurring. Restorative justice attempts to repair the relationships between the people involved in a harmful incident. This doesn't mean a return to normal for those involved, nor does it demand a strict 'forgiving' of the perpetrator by the victim, but allows for them to both continue to exist within their communities and seek reparation for the harm done to the victim–survivors. Restorative justice, however, is still an individualised response to harm: it works on individual bases and pays attention to the specifics of each situation. This is great, but it often fails to take into account systemic issues that caused the harm in the first place. For instance, restorative justice may seek to bring together a perpetrator and victim of sexual assault, for the perpetrator to apologise or compensate their victim and give back to their community in some way, for instance via community service.

What it misses out is what transformative justice brings in. Transformative justice seeks to address the direct harm caused whilst paying careful attention to the underlying dynamics and conditions that allowed them to happen. For example, male supremacy, class inequalities and white supremacy. Mia Mingus describes transformative justice, in a nutshell, as responding to violence and harm without creating more violence and harm. It's not just about individual instances of harm but also the wider picture. Transformative justice asks what causes harm to be enacted in the first place; what makes people want to hold power over others? This doesn't create excuses for perpetrators of violence, but instead acts as an explanation as to why the violence may have occurred in the first place; and having this explanation means we can try to change it. In transformative justice, a common path follows an 'accountability process', where survivors are first supported with specialised communities and given a space to heal in whatever way they see fit. Then, the other specialised community helps bring the perpetrators of violence to account, nurturing a space for them to realise their harmful behaviours and patterns, where they can both rectify previous harms and learn to not act in such ways in the future. The whole framework is one based not on punishment but on consequences. People can't just 'get away' with enacting violence on others, but instead will face tailored consequences, rather than ineffective blanket measures of punishment like prison. For example, they may lose their position of power over others, completely stop contact with the victim–survivor or attend classes to unlearn harmful behaviours towards women.

I've mentioned 'accountability' a few times – but what does that word actually mean? At its most literal level, it means being responsible to yourself and those around you for the choices you make and the consequences of those choices. In actuality, Elisabeth Long tells us that accountability can be incredibly variable. It can look like 'stopping harmful behavior, naming harmful behavior, giving sincere apologies, stepping down from leadership roles, developing daily healing and reflection practices to address root causes of harmful behavior, building a support pod, providing material repair, contributing to community efforts to end intimate and sexual harm'. Accountability can't be forced. We can't tell people that they must acknowledge the harm they've done – this shaming won't work to prevent harm occurring in the future. Instead, we must make seeking accountability something that people want to do. Imagine a scenario:

when someone has been told they assaulted someone, instead of immediately denying any wrongdoing, they seek to repair the damage caused, seek to help and rectify harm in appropriate ways. This world would look much more just than the denial and shame that is bred with our current justice systems.

Transformative justice seeks substantial healing for survivors: dedicated, personalised support groups and an acknowledging of their pain and rage. If the current criminal justice system hadn't organised my seeking of justice, and had I had faith that the man who assaulted me wouldn't have berated me, mocked me or gaslit me if I'd sought accountability directly from him, I would have felt a huge step in my healing to hear him say sorry, hear him acknowledge that how he acted deeply harmed me. If I'd have known he'd have got therapy, learned about rape culture, consent and the way patriarchy and ableism pervade all of our lives, then maybe I could have moved much further with my healing process. Maybe I wouldn't have been too afraid to be in London Bridge train station for two years afterwards, maybe I wouldn't still check his Twitter occasionally to check his movements aren't too close to mine. It wouldn't be fixed; it wouldn't be all better – but it would be better than it has been. We'd both have our dignity and I'd be able to move on with my life out of the direct orbit of that assault.

The one commonality between all the forms of justice, both criminal and transformative, is the length it takes – but instead of the years-long processes of collecting evidence, following bureaucracy, being cross-referenced in court and having an objective jury decide your fates, it's a long process of learning, acknowledging, processing and healing. It's justice based on survivor time; knowing it might take years for the survivor to be able to go through the process of addressing the harm, that they may have a breakdown and need to stop the process for six months, that they might not remember everything – and that's all OK.

As opposed to carceral feminism, abolition feminism advocates this seeking of transformative justice. It's a feminism that opposes violent state tactics of punishment and advocates community-based healing. Along with other abolitionist pursuits, transformative justice asks us to imagine the alternatives we want. If you could seek justice for your assaults, what would you really want? If you want them to be in prison, then why? The rage and the need for revenge is oh so real, but will my life really be helped if they spend the next ten years in prison (the answer may indeed be yes, if you're in direct, imminent danger), or if they lose all their friends and family?

I read books on abolitionist feminism and critiques of 'sex panics' and I find problems as a survivor – it hurts to read of the humanity of rapists when they took a part of our humanity from us. I feel unrelenting rage that they are given grace when none was given to us. But the kernels within those theories and books hold truth: revenge helps no one. As a survivor, learning about transformative justice is learning how to hold rage without adhering to the violence of state punishments. It's about learning to hold multiple complex feelings, truths, at once. I may believe in transformative justice, for my abusers to get therapy for their own traumas, and to learn

about consent and rape culture so they can become a
less harmful person, but I can also want them to suffer,
rotting in jail for the harm they did to me. These two
feelings can co-exist, as long as the ultimate goal ends
up helping the wider community. The latter feeling is
one of rightful rage. There is always a space carved out
in me for those feelings – they have driven me a long
way. Yet I know for wider society, and ultimately for
myself and my loved ones within it, the former inclina-
tions are what will really help society become more just
and move away from rape culture.

If you could imagine the most radical, most real conceptions of justice, what would that look like? We can start
now. Abolition and transformative justice don't mean we
have to immediately tear everything we currently have
down. Ruth Wilson-Gilmore says abolition of carceral
structures and the current oppressive world is about
'figuring out how to work with people to make something rather than figuring out how to erase something'.
It's about changing our current frameworks, how we
think about justice and how we enact those thoughts,
as opposed to just a breaking down of current systems.
Of course, at present, there are some cases in which
it is the safest option for the victim–survivors if their
perpetrators are confined – moving towards transformative justice doesn't strictly mean denying that. There are
plenty of steps we can take in the right direction, such as
non-reformist or abolitionist reforms. These are reforms
that will improve situations for victims, but that will not
strengthen the power of the state over both victims and
perpetrators. For example, activist and musician Annie

Tisshaw campaigned in 2020 to reduce the power the state had in demanding access to rape victims' therapy notes in criminal trials. This maintained the dignity of victims without enabling longer sentences or harsher punitive punishment for offenders.

Transformative justice isn't easy. It calls for a complete reimagining of how we see justice, and concurrently how we experience our world. It's complex and it's taxing. It's based on not reducing people to the singular harms they enact against others and not reducing people as solely victims of harm, devoid of agency. As sisters Adrienne Maree and Autumn Brown talk about on their podcast *How to Survive the End of the World*, such reductive thinking of 'good' and 'bad', 'victim' and 'perpetrator' is based on masculine, rationalist ideals of the binary. We must complicate our internal thinking about the world, in tow with the complication of the external world around us. This is all tiring – but it's also necessary. Transformative justice doesn't necessitate that survivors must interact with their abusers for the justice and accountability process, but instead that there are dedicated support groups provided to each person – a truly communal process of recovering from harm done. As opposed to the brutal, isolating burden of truth left at the feet of survivors in courts of law, a community approach helps seek honesty and accountability from those that have done harm, without re-traumatising survivors.

There are a lot of fancy social-justice terms being used, but transformative justice isn't just about the processes or technicalities. It's about changing our mindset in response to when harm occurs. It's about fostering the understanding and complexity to admit when we've done wrong. Even if you thought a sexual interaction was consensual, listen to what the other person involved is saying; their experience is theirs. Despite what we may want to believe (and oh, how I've wanted to believe), harm doers are still people, and the process of transformative justice acknowledges their humanity - that they are not solely bad people but, rather, complex people who have acted in ways that have gravely harmed others. This form of justice seeks to educate them about societal structures, ensure their support so they stay committed to the process and address any harm done to them in their own life that meant they were prone to acting in such ways. Such education and support will help people acknowledge that their actions seriously harmed someone, whilst also helping them avoid acting harmfully again by being attentive about consent and power dynamics. Natalie Fiennes writes, 'Prison provides an individualistic response to harm – it locates the problem in the body of the "bad" person rather than connecting patterns of harm to the conditions in which we live.' No one is wholly good or bad. We are complex, and all deserve help – for the benefit of our whole community.

Now, community is a big word. Community can mean lots of different things. At first thought, you may think of anything ranging from your country or your neighbourhood to where you go for 'community' meetings, to large identity groups or family networks. But community can literally mean the loved ones surrounding you. It doesn't have to be complex, formal or dependent on size. Your community could be you and two other people.

Elisabeth Long's earlier quote mentioned 'support pods'. The concept of pods was created because of the confusion around the word 'community'. Mia Mingus of the Bay Area Transformative Justice Collective (BATJC) defines each person's pod as 'made up of the people that you would call on if violence, harm or abuse happened to you; or the people that you would call on if you wanted support in taking accountability for violence, harm or abuse that you've done; or if you witnessed violence or if someone you care about was being violent or being abused'. This form of community is one based on intimate trust and relationships in our lives, rather than only state-based groups or activist organising structures. Your pod could include a trusted friend or family member, or someone you've only met a few times but had a deep understanding with. Instead of abstractly talking about some looming 'community' to turn to in the wake of harm, whether one has been a victim or a perpetrator, people can turn to those closest to them and begin to work out how to heal and be accountable. I, for one, have always chosen to tell friends and lovers about sexual violence I've experienced before turning to institutions for help. And, ultimately, it is my loved ones who have helped the most, validating me and caring for me.

Saying all this, though, we must pay attention to the fact that some people don't have any community; don't have anyone in their 'pods'. Many people, many survivors, are already isolated when abuse occurs. What if we don't have any good friends because we have severe social anxiety, or we've been isolated by our mobility issues, or we've been isolated because of the abuse itself? Transformative justice is often located in activist communities and with those who have already done a lot of work around healing and resistance. What about those who've never heard about it and don't have the resources to know how to access a form of transformative justice? Although there are some wonderful grassroots organisations across the UK, the move towards transformative justice often tends to be centralised in the USA as well. We need to see more education on the alternatives to normative justice, the alternatives to cruel modes of retributive justice. Perhaps as the generations change and more young people gain their knowledge online, society will move to acknowledge these other forms of justice and it will become normal for us to turn to these productive routes instead.

Thank you for the knowledge gained from everyone referenced in this chapter, to Kelsey and the rest of Cradle community, Mia Mingus, Ejeris Dixon, Leah Lakshmi Piepzna-Samarasinha, Mariame Kaba, Dr Gemma Ahearne and Mimi Kim.

For more information on transformative justice, and the processes I've mentioned, please see the bibliography for this chapter (p. 221–2).

# Chapter 14

# Fighting the Good Fight

This book has been pretty depressing for the most part. Our lives laced with sexual trauma are painful and this pain is made worse by the current structures of society. I never wanted to paint our experiences as reductively aspirational or inspirational, but I do want to give us some hope. The world is shit, but there are so many people trying to change that fact. There are so many people doing work at a grassroots level, working directly with survivors and interrupting the violence of the carceral state. Groups like Sisters Uncut, a feminist direct-action group fighting the Conservative government's austerity cuts to women's services. Austerity is the UK's Conservative government's approach to economic recovery – an approach which punches down and eviscerates public services including the NHS, fire services, local councils and survivors' services. The state of survivor-support services in the UK currently is pretty abysmal, to say the least. With services highly demanded and severely underfunded, a decade of austerity has hit survivors hard. Since 2010, thirty women's refuges have been closed as a direct result of austerity. Specialist survivors services, specifically dedicated to those from Black, Asian and Minority Ethnic (BAME) backgrounds, have been widely cut, with twenty-two of them having their funding cut since 2007. Funding cuts and reorganisations to benefits have also left survivors in vulnerable positions, especially as the main benefits system (Universal Credit) sees the money awarded to the highest earner in the house – a major problem if that happens to be an abusive partner. This means that many survivors are left stranded without help, oftentimes left within the abusive situations themselves, unable to escape.

I myself was let down by survivors' support services. Four months after reporting my assault to the police under the guidance of The Havens, I sought guidance from an ISVA (independent sexual violence advocate), someone who impartially helps you navigate the criminal justice system. The team at The Havens informed me that because my assault had happened over a year before, I wasn't eligible for assistance from their ISVAs. They had a meeting to decide if they could make 'an exception' for my case - they couldn't. I was left abandoned and rejected, left in the turmoil of a police investigation without the help I thought I'd been promised. Many of these support services do not adhere to survivor-time; do not adhere to the fact that you may at first refuse an ISVA, but after four months of a traumatising investigation, realise you desperately need one; they do not adhere to the fact that you won't seek help until seven months after the assault, won't make your statement until months again after that. The Havens told me to seek help from Rape Crisis, who can provide ISVAs after the one-year mark. I was on the waiting list for an ISVA from them for five months. In that time, I heard no updates, no indication of when I might receive help. I contacted them, and they'd simply tell me I was still on the waiting list. Within this time, I decided I wanted to withdraw my statement. I tried to seek any help I could find. I called random helplines for advocacy teams I can't remember the names of somewhere in the North of England and Wales. I was desperate for any information about the process; I was completely clueless. I had to take one of these calls during the induction party for my master's, scuttling away into the corner to talk about the investigation whilst my new cohort drank wine and made new friendships. I ultimately withdrew my statement without the help of a designated advocate, without anyone holding my hand and telling me what was really going to happen. I had to guess, and after that I was left reeling once again, with nothing to hold onto. That's why I created my website, my podcast and now this book. It wasn't for fun or creativity, although the latter was assuredly a by-product; it was primarily for survival. I'd felt so abandoned and stranded, I was determined to try and create something others like me could try to hold onto.

This brings us to who cares about survivors. Throughout this book we've seen various people care, whether that's in the form of transformative justice, deep friendships, people advocating for survivors or the people starting world movements against sexual violence. Almost all such people are women and feminine people. Almost all are oppressed and marginalised by their gender, many of them also by their race. We are socialised to care, to try and help whenever we can, and even when we can't. This caring is seen as free and limitless. When we volunteer at our local shelter, or work teaching consent classes, or create art or journalism to help others survive, it's not seen as 'real work', only as activism or advocacy. It's just a nice hobby on the side.

When I was creating my podcast, on numerous occasions when I would tell friends or acquaintances that I was 'going to work', they consistently assumed I meant my side-job of nannying. When I'd reaffirm to them that it was my work creating the podcast, they'd laugh in recognition, 'Oh yeah, I forget that's work!' Our societies don't see these pursuits as valuable work worthy of compensation. As well as sexual violence itself, the work against it is inherently gendered. This work is also often without boundaries. Such workers are seen as fair game – they are expected to be unlimited resources, talking whenever they're summoned and dealing with anger whenever it explodes from survivors. I myself have critiqued other advocates who have tried to help me, but who have ultimately not been able to because of institutional failures. Similarly, I myself have been critiqued by some for my place within what Leah Lakshmi Piepzna-Samarasinha has called the 'survivor-industrial-complex'. By this she means 'the web of institutions, practices, and beliefs that works to manage, contain, and offer resolution to survivors of sexual violence'. This complex operates on the understanding of the 'good' or 'fixed' survivor, the one who doesn't kick up too much of a fuss – the one, perhaps, who can placidly host a BBC podcast. Such critiques of the industry at large are indeed valid, yet the pressure that's often placed on the individual survivors working against rape culture seems unfair. The people most likely to do work against sexual violence are survivors who are women, and more specifically women of colour and/or queer women. This isn't just by choice – it's the only way many of us can survive. We have no other choice but to fight it ourselves when we shouldn't have to.

I have received countless social-media messages and emails about people's experiences with sexual violence, messages where they tell me I'm the only person they've ever told, if only through a pixelated screen. I feel touched when I receive these messages, feel overwhelmed with the impact my small work has had on some individuals' lives. Yet, it also feels wrong in many ways. Why do they feel they can only talk to me, a stranger they've never met? Why are our lives so disconnected that we feel so lonely without hearing one podcast desperately searched for in moments of distress? I am so glad that my work, and the work of many other activists, exists – but it seems fundamentally wrong that our struggling, traumatised selves have had to create the life rafts to keep us afloat. Where are the systems that propose to protect us? Where is the community care we so desperately need to survive? Why must it rest on the shoulders of the traumatised, the disabled, the crazy, the depressed, the depleted? Why must it rely on these already fading individuals, who will likely burn out and get compassion fatigue after years of being beaten down by the system? How has it come to be that those who often want to leave this poisonous world have to be the ones to care for it?

★

This was supposed to be a hopeful ending, wasn't it? After all I've just said, I do believe there is a way forward, and that way is to care. To care for our communities, our loved ones, and for those who are in even shittier situations than our own. No matter your identity, you can help others. If you're a survivor or not, if you're queer or not, if you're a person of colour or you're white, if you're anywhere on the gender spectrum, you will someday be in a position where you're better suited to stand up, to say no, than the person being affected by violence. If you're not a survivor and you see an instance of sexual violence occur – whether it's a rape joke or catcalling – realise that you may be the best person around you to intervene with such incidents. Likewise, if you're a white woman and you see a Black woman being sexually harassed by men, you are in the better position to stand up to them. It may be awkward, it may be scary, but it is better than standing by and doing nothing. To dismantle this rape culture we live in, we need to work together, we need to advocate for one another and educate younger ones about how to make this world a better place for everyone in it. We all have work to do.

I'm briefly going to start pointing fingers, though. The finger is pointing at men. Cis men, to be more precise. Men need to start fighting sexual violence more. Jackson Katz argues that to systematically prevent the abuse of power at the hands of men against women, we need to change our way of approaching the issue. Instead of sexual violence being seen as a woman's issue because that's the gender most likely to be affected by sexual violence, we need to start thinking of it as a man's issue because men are statistically the ones most likely to be perpetrating the violence. Advocacy and activism from women and other marginalised genders is needed to help us stay alive in the aftermath, but advocacy and activism by cis men is needed to prevent the violence from occurring in the first place. We need to teach our young men and boys to respect women, to learn about consent and how to be an active bystander. We need to teach men how to call each other in to discuss their harmful behaviours and work together to unlearn the toxic masculinity that's been forced upon them from a young age. Women and other people of marginalised genders do so much talking together about survival, rape culture and violent men; it is urgent time for men to start doing the same. We need to teach men to care and fight for this change on an equal level to the women in their lives.

There are so many people who already care. There's an ever-growing number of activists and creators fighting sexual violence and changing the way society thinks about the issue. Filmmakers like Michaela Coel, Jessica M. Thomson and Naima Ramos-Chapman; writers like Sohaila Abdulali, Leah Lakshmi Piepzna–Samarasinha, Amy Berkowitz, Lucia Osborne-Crowley, Chanel Miller, Roxane Gay, Winnie M Li, Ejeris Dixon and Lola Olufemi; artists like Emma Sulkowicz, Jen Brockman and Kara Walker. The scope of these creations speaks to the power that survivors step into when we can tell our own stories. We're beginning to see the complex truths that emerge when we survivors take control of representing our own lived experiences.

Countless individuals make up the communities that care, in the form of activist groups like Sisters Uncut, fighting austerity cuts affecting women, trans and non-binary survivors; Cradle Community, teaching people about transformative justice and centring young people of colour; My Body Back Project, a group of medical practitioners facilitating medical services tailored to women who are survivors; Clear Lines, an arts festival based in London exploring issues around sexual violence and consent; 100 Women I Know, a research, events and community group for survivors to feel less alone; Girls Against, a group of young activists against sexual harassment and assault occurring in live music spaces; The Good Lad Initiative, teaching young men and boys about consent and sexual violence; and Good Night Out, teaching venues and individuals how to be active bystanders and intervene in cases of sexual violence. There are also many individuals making waves in changing our society for survivors. Those like Shiori Ito, a Japanese journalist who brought a civil case against her rapist in Japan, and the musician FKA Twigs is fighting a legal battle against her alleged abuser; Usha Vishwakarma, founder of Red Brigade Lucknow, a self-defence programme for survivors; Refilwe Mooki, a poet and singer from Botswana fighting high rates of rape in the country; Denis Mukwege, a Congolese gynae-cologist who specialises in treating women who've been raped by militants; Nadia Murad, a human-rights lawyer held captive by the Islamic State, who fights the use of sexual violence as a weapon of war; Hello Rooster, a sex worker fighting sexual abuse and cover-ups in porn, especially those that occur on purportedly feminist ethical porn sets; Annie Tisshaw, a survivor who has campaigned against police access to victims' therapy notes in investigations; and Gaia Pope's family, who are still fighting for justice with an independent inquest into police conduct after her sexual assault and subsequent death. There are so many people who already care and will continue to care into our uncertain futures.

My experience can't and shouldn't be universalised, as it's just that – mine. I'm lucky to have been given a chance to project my voice to the world. What I hope will have resonated with others are the feelings and ideas at the heart of this complex topic.

If you're a survivor too, I hope you've found comfort in the rage and perseverance I have had. I want you to know that you didn't deserve what happened, and that it won't always be so dark. Know that you can be whatever you want to be: free, fatigued, unfathomably angry, hopeful, hopeless, damaged, scared, traumatised, happy, sexual, cynical, recovered, recovering. No one should be able to tell you how to feel. Read, journal, listen, watch, and hopefully one day you'll be able to work out how you feel about this confusing mess. There are so many people who want to support you and help you to persist.

For everyone else reading this who doesn't consider themselves a survivor – thank you. I hope you've found some illumination into what it's like living in this world as a survivor. I hope you feel moved to try and change it for us.

Society will not change overnight. Cruel men, cruel people and, most importantly, the cruel society that made them will not disappear tomorrow. All we can do is try to make things better, kinder. All we can do is care for one another, and I hope that this book will help in the movement to do that. All that matters is to care: for yourself, for those you love, and for the change that will come.

# Professional Resources

I always recommend talking to your loved ones about these painful circumstances, but I also recommend turning to professionals for help. For help in the aftermath of sexual violence, please consider contacting:

*(all 0800/0808 numbers, as well as all suicide hotlines, are **free** to contact.)

**For rape and sexual assault:**
Rape Crisis – rapecrisis.org.uk / 0808 802 9999
Rape Crisis Scotland – rapecrisisscotland.org.uk /0808 801 0302
The Havens (London) – https://www.thehavens.org.uk/ Imkaan (for BME survivors) – https://www.imkaan.org.uk/ / 020 7842 8525
Victim Support for Rape and Sexual Assault – 0808 168 9111
Women Against Rape – womenagainstrape.net
Women & Girls Network – www.wgn.org.uk / 0808 801 0660
The Survivors Trust – 08088 010818
Survivors' Network – 01273203380 / https://

survivorsnetwork.org.uk/get-help/
Survivors Library: https://survivorslibrary.org/

**For survivors of childhood sexual abuse:**
NAPAC: The National Association for People Abused
  in Childhood – 0808 801 0331 www.napac.org.uk
Safeline – https://www.safeline.org.uk/resources/
PODS: Positive Outcomes for Dissociative Survivors
A project of Survivors Trauma and Abuse Recovery Trust
  (START) – 0800 181 4420 / www.start-online.org.uk

**For male survivors:**
Survivors UK: Male Rape and Sexual Abuse Support
  – survivorsuk.org / 02035983898 / Webchat: help@
  survivorsuk.org
Safeline Male Survivors Helpline – 0808 800 5005 or
  text 07860 065187

**For LGBTQ+ survivors:**
Galop – 0800 999 5428 / http://www.galop.org.uk/
LGBTQ Switchboard (National Helpline) – 0300 330
  0630 (Daily, 10 a.m. to 10 p.m.)

**For those struggling with suicide or suicidal
thoughts or ideation:**
Samaritans – Call: 116 123 or email: jo@samaritans.org
Crisis Text Line – Text SHOUT to 85258
Papyrus Hopeline – Call: 0800 068 41 41 Text: 07860
  039 967
Email: pat@papyrus-uk.org

## For those supporting survivors:

MOSAC: Mothers of Sexually Abused Children – 0800 980 1958 / https://mosac.org.uk/

The Havens – Providing Support Help Page https://www.thehavens.org.uk/family-friends/ providing-support/

Survivors' Network: 'Supporting Survivors of Sexual Assault'

https://survivorsnetwork.org.uk/resource/ supporting-survivors-of-sexual-assault/

# Further Reading

**Books**

Abdulali, Sohaila. *What We Talk About When We Talk About Rape.*

Angelou, Maya. *I Know Why the Caged Bird Sings.*

Bean, Lexie (ed.). *Written on the Body.*

Beilin, Caren. *Blackfishing the IUD.*

Berkowitz, Amy. *Tender Points.*

Cvetkovich, Anne. *Depression: A Public Feeling.*

Daley-Ward, Yrsa. *The Terrible.*

Davis, Angela Y. *Women, Race and Class.*

Dixon, Ejeris and Lakshmi-Piepzna Samarasinha. *Beyond Survival.*

Fowles, Stacey May and Lee, Jen Sookfong. *Whatever Gets You Through.*

Fiennes, Natalie. *Behind Closed Doors: Sex Education Transformed.*

Gay, Roxane. *Not That Bad.*
*Hunger.*
*Bad Feminist.*
*An Untamed State.*

Hedva, Johanna. *Sick Woman Theory.*

Huber, Sonya. *Pain Woman Takes Your Keys (and other essays from a nervous system).*

Kasbeer, Sarah. *A Woman, A Plan, An Outline of a Man.*

Lakshmi-Piepzna Samarasinha. *Care Work: Dreaming Disability Justice.*

Long, Amy. *Codependence.*

Lorde, Audre. *Your Silence Will Not Protect You.* (Silverpress)

Mailhot, Terese Marie. *Heart Berries.*

Miller, Chanel. *Know My Name.*

Montell, Amanda. *Wordslut.*

Osborne-Crowley, Lucia. *I Choose Elena.*

Olufemi, Lola. *Feminism, Interrupted.*

Sudjic, Olivia. *Exposure.*

Thom, Kai Cheng. *I Hope We Choose Love: A Trans Girl's Notes from the End of the World.*

Vanasco, Jeannie. *Things We Didn't Talk About When I was a Girl.*

Van der Kolk, Bessel. *The Body Keeps the Score.*

Verso. *Where Freedom Starts: Sex Power Violence #MeToo.*

Weijun-Wang, Esmé. *The Collected Schizophrenias.*

## Podcasts

*After: Surviving Sexual Assault.* Catriona Morton, BBC Sounds.

*Silent Waves.* Raquel O'Brien and Georgina Savage.

*Obsessed with . . . I May Destroy You.* Sophie Duker, BBC Sounds.

*Bodies.* Allison Behringer, KCRW.

*Chronic.* Lucy Pasha-Robinson, HuffPost UK.

*How to Survive the End of the World.* Autumn Brown and adrienne maree brown.

*The Heart.* Radiotopia.

*Trauma Queen.* Jimanekia Eborn.
*Vulnerable Podcast.* Allysa Rochelle.

## Websites

*Bloom* is a free, web-based support service run by Chayn. Designed for anyone who is currently experiencing or has experienced domestic and sexual abuse, support is offered via 5 courses. bloom.chayn.co/

*CHAYN* is a global volunteer network addressing gender-based violence by creating intersectional survivor-led resources online. chayn.co/

*Life Continues After* is a survivor-centred arts platform sharing the words, sounds and sights that have helped survivors cope. lifecontinuesafter.com

*The Ins and Outs of Consent.* The Face Magazine x Galdem x BBC. theface.com/gal-dem/ imaydestroyyou

*The Radical Resilience Project.* RRP is a fund, a mutual support space, a space for learning and a space for challenging the systems built to oppress us. www.theradicalresilienceproject.org

*The Survivors Network:* 'Resources' . survivorsnetwork. org.uk/resources/

## Instagram

@elyssa_rider
@guerilla_feminist
@iamrukiat
@justice4sexualassault
@youlookokaytome
@prishita_eloise

@thespeakupspace
@supporting_women_as_men
@alokvmenon
@uglyinahotway
@babeworld3000
@ablezine
@helloachemagazine
@asickmagazine
@sicksadgirlz
@brittfrank
@remembering_comfort_women
@mia.mingus
@iharterika
@thechroniciconic
@survivorslibrary
@thegeminiproj
@cute.cartel
@unapologeticallysurviving
@survivorarts
@rubyrare

# Chapter Notes

## Introduction
Angela Y. Davis, *Women, Race and Class*, Penguin Classics, 3rd October 2019

## Part 1: Language and Definitions

*Chapter 1. The Infinite Grey*
Carr, A.P., Smith F. *Sexual Offences Act 2003*
Ministry of Justice, Office for National Statistics and Home Office (2013). *An Overview of Sexual Offending in England Wales*.
Kelly, L. (1988). *Surviving Sexual Violence*.
Cho, Grace M. (2019). *Listening to Silence/Hearing Voices: The Irrational as Memory Work* [lecture].
Vaid Menon, A. (2019). *Never Their Own, Always His.* https://www.alokvmenon.com/blog
Hedva, J. (2015) *Sick Woman Theory*.

*Chapter 2. What Rape Isn't (though sometimes it is)*
Shara, N. *Facing Shame: From Saying Sorry to Doing Sorry* in *Beyond Survival* AK Press, 2nd April 2020.
Yuknavitch, L. *The Chronology of Water* Canongate Books, 2nd January 2020.

*Chapter 3. Kiss Chase*

Beilin, C *Blackfishing the IUD* Wolfman Books, 17th October 2019.

Legislation.gov.uk. 2010. Equality Act 2010. [online]

Plan UK – Street Harassment. https://plan-uk.org/
act-for-girls/street-harassment.

Alexandra Topping, *Guardian*. 'Almost all young women in
the UK have been sexually harassed, survey finds' https://
www.theguardian.com/world/2021/mar/10/almost-
all-young-women-in-the-uk-have-been-sexually-har-
assed-survey-finds

Montell, A, *Wordslut* HarperWave, 9th July 2020.

Gordon-Smith, Eleanor. *This American Life* [podcast]

Department for Education, UK Government 2019.
*Relationships and Sex Education (RSE): Guidance.*

Big Talk Education. https://www.bigtalkeducation.co.uk/
bigtalk-education/

Come Curious. YouTube. https://www.youtube.com/c/
ComeCurious/featured

Hannah Witton. YouTube. https://www.youtube.com/
channel/UC6iWKC08iw9K-R6Wh5pbZNQ

Brown Girls Do It Too. *BBC Sounds*. [podcast]

Jimanekia Eborn. *Trauma Queen*. [podcast]

Ruby Rare. Instagram @rubyrare


# Part 2: Politics

*Chapter 4 The Hashtag*

Cwiek, Sarah. 'After ten years, Detroit rape kit backlog
cleared, but still "a long way to go"'. Michigan Radio.

[Begrudgingly included for the sake of comprehensive cita-
tion] Flanagan, Caitlin. 'The Humiliation of Aziz Ansari'
*The Atlantic*. [article]

Kelly, Liz., Lovett, Jo and Regan, Lina. *A gap or a chasm? Attrition in reported rape cases.*

Me too. Movement (https://metoomvmt.org/)

Middle Ground. 'Has The #MeToo Movement Gone Too Far?'. YouTube.

Phipps, Alison. *Me, Not You.* Manchester University Press, 6th April 2020

The Open University. *Here's the Truth About False Accusations of Sexual Violence.* [article]

Warwick, William, 'Woody Allen Is Not a Monster. He Is a Person. Like My Father.' *Gawker.* [article]

[Begrudgingly included for the sake of comprehensive citation] Weiss, Bari. 'Aziz Ansari Is Guilty. Of Not Being a Mind Reader.' *New York Times.*

*Chapter 5. Intersections of Violence*

A Verso Report. *Where Freedom Starts: Sex Power Violence #MeToo.*

Bailey, Moya and Trudy aka @thetrudz. *On misogynoir: citation, erasure, and plagiarism.*

Bean, Lexie (ed.); foreword and additional pieces by Dean Spade, Nyala Moon, Alex Valdes, Sawyer DeVuyst and Ieshai Bailey. *Written on the Body: Letters from Trans and Non-Binary Survivors of Sexual Assault and Domestic Violence.* Jessica Kingsley Publishers, 21st March 2018

Crenshaw, Kimberle. *Mapping the Margins: Intersectionality, Identity Politics, and Violence against Women of Color.* [article]

*The Urgency of Intersectionality.* TED talk.

Dalton, Jane. 'Murdered and missing women and girls in Canada tragedy is genocide rooted in colonialism, official inquiry finds.' *Independent.* [article]

Epstein, Rebecca., Blake, Jamilia J., González, Thalia.

Georgetown Law Centre on Poverty and Equality. *Girlhood Interrupted: The Erasure of Black Girls' Childhood.* [article]

Hamad, Ruby. *White Tears/Brown Scars: How White Feminism Betrays Women of Colour.* Trapeze, 22nd October 2020.

Lorde, Audre. 'Learning from the 60s'. *Sister Outsider: Essays and Speeches.* Penguin Classics, 4th July 2019

Fannie Lou Hamer 'Nobody's Free Until Everybody's Free,' Speech Delivered at the Founding of the National Women's Political Caucus, Washington, D.C., 10 July 1971

Imkaan https://www.imkaan.org.uk/

Sistah Space https://www.sistahspace.org/

National Organisation for Women (NOW). *The Disability Community & Sexual Violence.* [article]

Office for National Statistics. Sexual offences in England and Wales: year ending March 2017.

Owl. 'Excluding trans women from safe, same-sex spaces puts their lives at risk.' *Metro Online.* [article]

Pham, Xoai. 'What This Trans Survivor Wants J.K. Rowling to Know.' *Autostraddle.* [article]

Phipps, Alison. *Me, Not You.*

Smith, Valerie. 'Split Affinities: The Case of Interracial Rape' in *Conflicts in Feminism.* Routledge, 7th March 1991

Southern Poverty Law Center. 'Sexual Abuse/Discrimination.' *Under Siege: Life for Low-Income Latinos in the South.* 2009. [article]

Them. 'Trans Women Open Up About Their #MeToo Sexual Assault Experiences.' YouTube.

Truth, Sojourner. *Ain't I A Woman?* [Speech 1851]

Westbrook, Laurel and Schilt, Kristen. 'Doing Gender, Determining Gender: Transgender People, Gender Panics, and the Maintenance of the Sex/Gender/Sexuality System.' *Gender and Society* 2014.

## Part 3: Minds and Bodies

*Chapter 6. A Complex Condition*

Medical News Today. *What is Complex PTSD?*
https://www.medicalnewstoday.com/
articles/322886#what-is-complex-ptsd

Trade Union Congress (2018). Breaking Point: the crisis in mental health funding.

Royal College of Psychiatrists. Two-fifths of patients waiting for mental health treatment forced to resort to emergency or crisis services.

SafeBAE: Safe Before Anyone Else. (Safebae.org)

Sontag, Susan. *Illness as Metaphor.* Penguin Classics, 3rd July 2009

Van der Kolk, B. *The Body Keeps the Score.* Penguin, 24th September 2015


*Chapter 7. What Our Bodies Tell Us*

Barker, Kristin. *The Fibromyalgia Story.* Temple University Press, 17th August 2005

Burke-Harris, N. *How Childhood Trauma Affects Health Across a Lifetime.* TED talk.

Ciccone D.S., Elliott D.K., Chandler H.K., Nayak S. Raphael K.G. Sexual and physical abuse in women with fibromyalgia syndrome: a test of the trauma hypothesis. *Clin J Pain.* 2005.

Clare, Eli. *Brilliant Imperfect: Grappling with Cure.* Duke University Press Books, 3rd February 2017

Dusenbery, Maya. *Doing Harm* HarperOne, Reprint edition, 18th April 2019.

Hedva, Johanna. *Sick Woman Theory.*

Lampe, A. MD; Sölder, E. MD; Ennemoser, A. MD; Schubert, C. MD; Rumpold, G. PhD; Söllner, W.

MD. Chronic Pelvic Pain and Previous Sexual Abuse, *Obstetrics & Gynecology*: December 2000.

Lazard, Carolyn. *How to be a Person in the Age of Autoimmunity.* [article]

Lev-Wiesel Rachel, Bechor Yair, Daphna-Tekoah Shir, Hadanny Amir, Efrati Shai. *Brain and Mind Integration: Childhood Sexual Abuse Survivors Experiencing Hyperbaric Oxygen Treatment and Psychotherapy Concurrently.* 2018.

Nelson, Maggie. *The Argonauts* Melville House, 7th April 2016.

Orr-Andrawes, Alison MD. *The Case of Anna O.: A Neuropsychiatric Perspective.* [article]

Osborne-Crowley, Lucia. *I Choose Elena* The Indigo Press, 19th September 2019.

Paul Ingraham. *Chronic Pain and Tragic Irony: I started out helping people with chronic pain and now I have it.* [article]

Scarry, Elaine. *The Body in Pain.* Oxford University Press, 23rd April 1987

Stewart, Conor. *Share of disability in the United Kingdom (UK) in 2018/19, by age and gender.*

Van der Kolk, B. *The Body Keeps the Score.*

Versus Arthritis. *£24 million secured to lead the way in pain research in the UK.*

Verywell Mind. *What Is Hysteria? The Past and Present.* [article]

*Chapter 8. The Ways We Cope*

Laguna Treatment Hospital. *Trauma and Alcohol Addiction.* [article]

Posttraumatic Stress Disorder and Alcohol Dependence in Young Women. *Journal of Studies on Alcohol and Drugs.*

Liebschutz, Jane et al. 'The relationship between sexual and physical abuse and substance abuse consequences.' *Journal of substance Abuse Treatment.*

Noll, J. G. et al 'Revictimization and Self-Harm in Females Who Experienced Childhood Sexual Abuse: Results from a Prospective Study', *Journal of Interpersonal Violence*.

National Eating Disorder Association. *Trauma, Sexual Assault & Eating Disorders*.

VeryWellMind. The Influence of Abuse and Trauma on Eating Disorders.

Allyn, Pam. *Reading is Like Breathing in; Writing is Like Breathing out*.

Kafer, Alison. *Feminist, Queer, Crip* Indiana University Press, 9th July 2013.

Fazeli, Taraneh. Notes for 'Sick Time, Sleepy Time, Crip Time: Against Capitalism's Temporal Bullying' in conversation with the Canaries.

## Part 4: Relationships

*Chapter 9. All I Know of Sex*

*Chapter 10. On Needing Each Other*
Berkowitz, Amy. *Tender Points* Timeless, Infinite Light, 20th June 2015.

https://www.attachmentproject.com/blog/avoidant-attachment-style/

Holzer, Jenny. (1993) *it is in your self-interest to find a way to be very tender*.

Nelson, Maggie. *The Red Parts* Vintage, 1st June 2017.

*Chapter 11. A Short Word on Forgiveness*

## Part 5: Justice

*Chapter 12. The Criminal Justice System*

Big Brother Watch. 'End Digital Strip Searches.', *Campaigns*.

Chloe, as told to Sirin Kale. 'My Abuser Used My Therapy Notes Against Me During His Trial'. *Vice*. [article]

Davies, Caroline. 'Woman was killed by ex-lover just days after police seized her phone'. *Guardian*. [article]

Fisher, Megan. 'Rape social media posts: How speaking out got twin sisters sued. BBC. [article]

Kale, Sirin. 'Rape Victims Are Being Told They Can't Go to Therapy'. *Vice*. [article]

Metropolitan Police. 'What is Rape and Sexual Assault?', *Advice and Information*.

Moloney, Liv. 'Off Limits: Is Rape the Perfect Crime?' *Sky News*. [article]

Rights of Women. *Reporting an Offence to the Police: A Guide to Criminal/Police Investigations*. 2014.

Topping, Alexandra and Barr, Caelainn. 'Rape convictions fall to record low in England and Wales.' *Guardian*. [article]

*Chapter 13. A Brief Introduction to Transformative Justice*

Brown, Adrienne Maree. 'What is/isn't Transformative Justice' in *Beyond Survival*.

Davis, Angela Y. *Women, Race and Class*. Penguin Classics, 3rd October 2019

Dixon, Ejeris and Lakshmi Piepzna–Samarasinha, Leah. *Beyond Survival: Strategies and Stories from the Transformative Justice Movement*.

Fiennes, Natalie. *Behind Closed Doors*. Pluto Press, 20th September 201

Froio, Nicole. 'Non-carceral approaches to #MeToo.' *Academic Feminista, Medium*. [article]

https://medium.com/academica-feminista/
non-carceral-approaches-to-metoo-12a4479e0406

Long, Elisabeth. 'Vent diagrams as healing practice: TJ Tips
from the Overlap' from *Beyond Survival*.

Miller, Chanel. *Know My Name*. Viking, 3rd September 2020

Mingus, Mia (for the BATJC). Pods and Podmapping
Worksheet. https://batjc.wordpress.com/
pods-and-pod-mapping-worksheet/

Mingus, Mia. 'Transformative Justice: A Brief Description'.
*Leaving Evidence* [blog]

Petitjean, Clément. 'Prisons and Class Warfare: An Interview
with Ruth Wilson Gilmore'. Verso Books Website.

Press, Alex. '#MeToo Must Avoid 'Carceral Feminism'.'
*Vox*. [article]

*Survived and Punished*. https://survivedandpunished.org/

Tisshaw, Annie. 'My Rape Case Was Dropped – I'm Not
Surprised Conviction Rates Are Low'. *Vice*.

*Transform Harm*. https://transformharm.org/

## Part 6: Conclusion

*Chapter 14. Fighting the Good Fight*

Katz, Jackson. *Violence Against Women – It's a Men's Issue*.
TED talk.

Lakshmi Piepzna-Samarasinha, Leah. 'Not Over It, Not
Fixed, and Living a Life Worth Living' from *Whatever Gets
You Through*. Read the excerpt online: https://www.vice.
com/en/article/bj9gpm/not-over-it-not-fixed-and-living-
a-life-worth-living-whatever-gets-you-through

# Acknowledgments

First of all, I want to thank myself, for surviving and living through the bullshit to write this book.

Thank you to my amazing commissioning editor Marleigh Price for her belief in me and my wonderful agent Rachel Mann for all her support.

Thank you to the Society of Authors' Authors Foundation grant, which allowed me to relax financially for a little bit whilst writing.

Thank you to the lovely humans who proofread parts of this book whilst it was gestating: Alba Donnachie, Kirsty Nolan, Ella Asheri, Urvashi Aarti Panchal, Indigo Ayling, Charlotte J. Fitz, Catherine Mosley, Henri Lau. Fiona Daglish is the brilliant on-call doctor and for ever friend I mention (thanks for always being a text or phone call away for the past twelve years).

Thank you to my production team for the podcast *After*: Danielle Stephens, Gabriela Jones, Rachel Simpson, Claire Chadwick, Ella Woods, Alice Lloyd. Without all of you, I wouldn't be where I am in my budding career. (Having a chain of command comprised only of women did wonders for my confidence in the industry.) Gratitude to all of the guests who featured on the podcast – it wouldn't be what it is without any of you, and you have helped so many survivors in their ways of coping.

Sending love and admiration to all the survivors who've reached out to me, to those who've contributed to Life Continues After and to those who've listened to my honesty on the podcast.

To the people whose stories I mention or allude to throughout, I see you and thank you for letting me use your experiences.

I have endless admiration and gratitude to the people doing the real work in Transformative Justice, disability justice and grassroots advocacy for survivors – without your knowledge sharing, I wouldn't be the writer (or person) I am today. The knowledge featured throughout this book is owed to countless feminists, thinkers and writers I've been influenced by. Many Black feminist and woman of colour feminist scholars: Audre Lorde, Angela Y. Davis, Kimberle Crenshaw, Sara Ahmed, Lola Olufemi; Crip and disabled thinkers and writers: Leah Lakshmi Piepzna–Samarasinha, Eli Clare, Mia Mingus, Alison Kafer and Sami Schalk; and authors of medical patriarchy and trauma studies: Maya Dusenbery, Caren Beilin, Johanna Hedva and Amy Berkowitz.

Thank you to the dialogues I've had with writers I so admire: Alison Phipps, Amy Berkowitz, Lucia Osborne-Crowley – it astonishes me that I'm starting to move in the circles of writers and thinkers I admire so much.

Thank you to my kind co-workers at Goldsmiths Students' Union: Jo Swo, Lou Kendaru, Elizabeth George, Aarti Panchal, Avery Delaney and Cade Anderson-Smith – and to our trainers at Rape Crisis South London.

I'm forever grateful to my friend and academic supervisor at Goldsmiths, Akanksha Mehta – the world would be a better place if everyone had a teacher like you.

I also must give a shout-out to Phoebe Bridgers for releasing the album *Punisher* to coincide with the writing of this book. Your voice shouting 'the end is near' has spurred me on throughout.

To Mum and Dad, thank you for all your devoted support over the years, for your help with my struggles and for your unwavering belief in me.

To my chosen family: Alba, Yingbi, Indigo, Kirsty, Joy. You've all kept me alive in more ways than you know. Thank you to lovely friends: Henri Lau, Morven Loh, Enya Sullivan, Taylor Gardener, Ella Asheri, Maymana Arefin, Sanjana Varghese, Giannina Rodriguez-Rico, Catherine Mosley, Charlie Ponzio, Gabriela Jones, Camilla van Herwijnen, Maggie Matić, Fiona Daglish and Sammie Margetson. And, the men I trust: Tom Madden, Sam Lawton, Jake Vaughan, Ted Fenton, Rory Gradon, Luc Wilkinson. Thanks for giving me some hope in cis masculinity.

To my love, Jamie, thanking you for holding me when I need it. I love you and I'm grateful we've had each other through the storms.

My beautiful little dog Lina, you make me feel so safe, especially when you lay by my side through the pain, and my childhood dog Jack – you're the only reason I hold out hope for an afterlife.

# Credits

Catriona Morton and Trapeze would like to thank everyone at Orion who worked on the publication of *The Way We Survive*.

**Editorial**
Marleigh Price

**Copy editor**
Sarah Hulbert

**Proofreader**
Claire Wallis

**Audio**
Paul Stark
Amber Bates

**Contracts**
Anne Goddard
Jake Alderson

**Design**
Debbie Holmes
Joanna Ridley
Nick May

**Editorial Management**
Jane Hughes

**Finance**
Jasdip Nandra
Afeera Ahmed
Elizabeth Beaumont
Sue Baker

**Marketing**
Brittany Sankey

**Production**
Claire Keep

**Publicity**
Francesca Pearce

**Sales**
Jennifer Wilson
Esther Waters
Victoria Laws

Frances Doyle
Georgina Cutler

**Operations**
Jo Jacobs
Sharon Willis
Lisa Pryde
Lucy Brem

# Help us make the next generation of readers

We – both author and publisher – hope you enjoyed this book. We believe that you can become a reader at any time in your life, but we'd love your help to give the next generation a head start.

Did you know that 9 per cent of children don't have a book of their own in their home, rising to 13 per cent in disadvantaged families*? We'd like to try to change that by asking you to consider the role you could play in helping to build readers of the future.

We'd love you to think of sharing, borrowing, reading, buying or talking about a book with a child in your life and spreading the love of reading. We want to make sure the next generation continue to have access to books, wherever they come from.

And if you would like to consider donating to charities that help fund literacy projects, find out more at **www.literacytrust.org.uk** and **www.booktrust.org.uk**.

THANK YOU

*As reported by the National Literacy Trust